Jagular Goes Everywhere

Jagular
Goes Everywhere

(mis)Adventures in a $300 Sailboat

by
Tom Pamperin

CEDAR STREET PRESS

Published 2014 by
Cedar Street Press
P.O. Box 414
Chippewa Falls, WI 54729

ISBN-13: 978-0-9914617-1-4
Library of Congress Control Number: 2014907079

Typeset by Lodestar Editorial
Printed by Worzalla, Stevens Point, WI

Portions of "Jagular Gets Rescued," "Jagular in the North Woods," and "Jagular Goes South" first appeared online at www.duckworks-magazine.com. Portions of "Jagular at Swan Lake," "Jagular's Wild Ride," and "Jagular's North Channel Adventure" first appeared in *Small Craft Advisor*.

The author is grateful to David Brazer and Mara Brazer for permission to include brief selections from *Well Favored Passage: A Guide to Lake Huron's North Channel* by Marjorie Cahn Brazer. Revised edition, published by Peach Mountain Press, 1983.

Drawings by Eric D. Bott

For Cathy (of course)

Contents

'What do Jagulars do?' asked Piglet,
hoping that they wouldn't.

A. A. Milne, *The House at Pooh Corner*

Foreword

I love small boats. For me they embody the very essence of adventure and a real connection with the elements. What's more, a small boat can be a magic carpet that carries the spirit as well as the body to magical places inaccessible in any ordinary manner.

I've been high in the rigging of majestic tall ships, helmed amazingly fast ocean racers battling with the elements far offshore, sailed in world cruisers able to cope with everything that the sea can throw at them as they sailed toward distant and exotic ports, and worked on sailing freighters reeking with history and tradition. But nothing, nothing at all touches my soul in the same way as creeping up a narrow channel in a very small open boat, exploring the thin narrow places where others can't go.

In a small boat, fighting my way around a point against wind and tide is an adventure akin to rounding Cape Horn in the world cruiser. Sailing across to a port fifteen miles from my starting point to go ashore and treat myself to an ice cream is akin to voyaging afar on the tall ship. Sneaking up on a (slightly) bigger yacht by cutting across the shallows gives me more of a kick than ocean racing. And as for the freighter? I'm hugely proud of the day that I was able to use my small plywood yawl to deliver some spare engine parts to a friend whose motor yacht had broken down while cruising.

All of this is so personal, so close a fit, and involves such an intimate connection with the elements and the boat, that it can be extremely difficult to communicate to others. But

Tom Pamperin is able to do just that, something that makes his writing very special.

I first encountered Tom's work when I read an early version of "Jagular Goes South" in Chuck Leinweber's online magazine, Duckworks. In that story I met Jagular, the infamous Raspberry Newtons, the oystershell banks and the errant shirt. I loved the descriptions of the thrills and misadventures, the fear and exhilaration, the peace and beauty to be found sailing on what was, for a small boat, big waters. I empathized with the writer's fears, felt again the joys, and sympathized with the painful lessons learned. "Been there, done that," comes to mind. Wonderful stuff. I've wanted to participate in the Texas 200 ever since.

Much to my surprise, some time later I had an email from Tom, who was writing a story about me and my design work for a major boating magazine. We had the chance to meet at the Port Townsend Wooden Boat Festival, and later we managed to spend quite a few hours sailing together at Sail Oklahoma, where I was pleased to show Tom some tricks. We share a lot of interests and I'm privileged to know him as a friend.

Tom has a rare talent: he's able to capture the whole of the experience most of us know from the classic words of Kenneth Grahame: "There is nothing— absolutely nothing— half so much worth doing as simply messing about in boats." Those words are wonderful, inspiring, almost spiritual.

The stories in this book convey that reality. You'll shake your head; I did. You'll grin and nod; I did. You'll say "Ouch, that must have hurt;" I did. And you'll laugh—I did!

John Welsford
Hamilton
New Zealand

Prologue

At one point in my life I left the tall pines and rock-studded rivers of northern Wisconsin to live along a marshy tallgrass finger of the Atlantic. From the dock behind my house I could watch the sun rise over the open ocean and hear the cry of the wheeling gulls, and I expected to develop a mysterious and satisfying communion with the sea. But the sea felt like sandpaper and smelled like low tide, and the gulls were no different from the ones that inhabited the landfills and parking lots back home. Barnacles covered everything that wasn't already covered with slime, and packs of horseshoe crabs scuttled hideously along the shore like monstrous ravaging trilobites. My wife would wander the beach for hours looking for water-worn glass and colorful pebbles. I would wander the beach for about ten minutes and wonder where all the trees were. Then I'd go eat breakfast.

Gradually, though, I learned to love the sea. I even became something of an open-ocean swimmer, because once when I was wandering the beach on a military installation late at night some MPs came to arrest me and I swam away instead. The MPs gestured angrily and shouted at me and swept their big spotlight across the waves trying to keep me in sight until I swam far out into the open sea, out of sight of land. I kept swimming for so long afterwards that it became a habit. I always swam in the dark because it was easier to ignore the sharks.

"You only swam in the dark a few times," Jagular interrupts.

"Quiet," I tell him. "You're not in the story yet."

"And there weren't any sharks," he goes on, ignoring me as usual.

"There might have been sharks," I insist. "Besides, you haven't even been built yet. Just let me tell this part my way."

"When does the part about me start?"

"Pretty soon," I tell him.

"Good," he says. "That's the best part."

Anyway, I did a lot of swimming and saw some MPs, and it seemed like they were always angry about something or other. There may not have been any sharks or spotlights. But if you're the kind of reader who insists on holding rigidly to the facts while ignoring the shadow of the larger truths behind them, this may not be the book for you. And either way, I still wasn't a sailor or a boat builder.

But the romance of the sea proved inescapable, even after I moved back to the north woods, so I started building a twenty-foot yawl in my dining room one day while my wife was away at work. I worked on the mizzen mast first because it was the only part of the boat that would fit in the house. I didn't even finish it. On paper the mizzen mast was made of straight lines; in reality, it wasn't.

Eventually I dragged the partially assembled mast out to the derelict shed in our backyard—the carriage house, our real estate agent called it, somehow managing to keep a straight face—and started spending my time reading about boats instead of trying to build them. I read books by Webb Chiles and Robin Lee Graham and Joshua Slocum; I read books by Bernard Moitessier and Tristan Jones. I read *Fastnet, Force 10* and *The Strange Last Voyage of Donald Crowhurst* and *Two Years Before the Mast*. I spent days dreaming of the lonely limitless sea where I would wear bulky cable-knit sweaters and drink hot tea and wake up each morning with flying fish flopping on the deck and albatrosses soaring overhead. I'd pull out my battered sextant for a noon sight every day and carefully draw circles and LOPs and running fixes and bearings and other cryptic marks on the chart. Then I'd look at the clouds and glance at the compass and test the wind by licking my finger and holding it up to see which side felt cool, and I'd stare with squinty eyes at all the lines on the charts and wonder whether it would be better to round Cape Horn or submit to an undignified slog through the Panama Canal.

Between books I started going to auctions and bidding on leaky-bilged deep-keeled ocean cruisers, boats whose best days were so far behind them even I could barely convince myself they'd ever existed. My older brother, with a firmer grasp on reality, suggested that it might be better to start smaller, maybe a quick-build beach cruiser with a flat bottom and plywood sides. I'll build one, too, he promised. We'll each pick a design and build them together, finish them in a couple of weekends. Temporary boats, he said. Just until we decide what we really want.

"I'm a temporary boat?" Jagular interrupts again, looking over my shoulder as I type.

"We're all temporary," I tell him. "Some of us are just more temporary than others."

I did my best to make Jagular as temporary as I could, actually, wanting to move on to that deep-keeled ocean cruiser as soon as possible. I tried to buy cheap luan plywood for the hull but misread the stickers at the lumberyard and brought home some better stuff by mistake—five plies, no voids, glue that looked like it might be at least water-resistant. To make up for my mistake with the plywood, I used a cheap polyurethane adhesive that even the manufacturer refused to claim would hold up to full immersion.

But however temporary he might turn out to be, Jagular had a solid pedigree, I knew; his lines were drawn by the great

Phil Bolger, who included the plans in his classic book *Boats With An Open Mind*. That's where I found my boat: Chapter 22, design 542—the Pirate Racer.

Pirate Racer! When I first read the name I could almost hear the tropic breezes stirring the coconut palms overhead; the crying of the seagulls, the roar of the surf; booming cannons and ringing cutlasses, tattered maps and shining pieces of eight; fair winds, long passages, and endless horizons. No matter that design 542 was a small flat-bottomed skiff hardly big enough to fit two adults aboard in even the calmest conditions. This would be my boat, I decided.

"*That's* the boat?" my brother said when I showed him the plans.

"That's it," I told him.

He looked at the drawings again, shook his head. "Well," he said finally. "It should be pretty easy to build."

Jagular Goes Everywhere

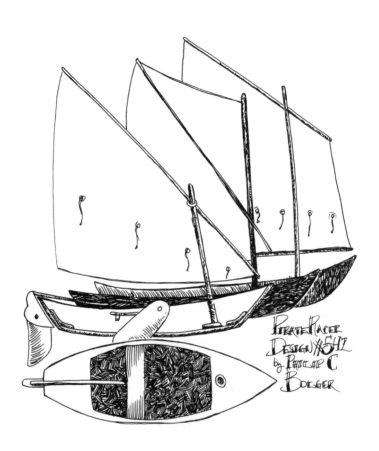

Pirate Racer
Design X542
by Phillip C
Bolger

Pirate Racer!

Jagular Sets Sail

IF IT WEREN'T FOR MY BROTHER I'd have never even gotten started with this sailing nonsense, I remind myself in a fit of annoyance, having just mis-cut the bevel on the starboard chine log again. I could be safely at home curled up on the couch with my wife and cat. But here we are, with no wife or cat in sight, building a boat in my brother's garage. We're working from blurry photocopies of the plans in Phil Bolger's book *Boats With An Open Mind*, and the accompanying instructions are almost impossible to read because the original plans were printed on sheets of paper the size of a kitchen table, and in the book the drawings have been reduced to the size of my hand. I guess at a lot of the numbers and make the rest up. But with my brother helping—well, with him building and me helping—we get the shapes mostly right, and the hull comes together quickly in his garage: sides, bottom, decks, bulkheads, and a layer of fiberglass cloth. Pretty soon we load the boat on a trailer for the drive home and then before I know it I'm finishing the boat alone in my own driveway.

"By guess and by God," I tell the boat as I trim each ill-fitting piece and jam it in place. "That's how the old-timers did it. No worrying about measurements and so on."

"Uh-huh," the boat says. Not even launched yet and already a critic. "You've read the plans, haven't you?"

"Plans?" I say. "Good builders never pay much attention to the plans."

"Good builders, no."

I don't bother to answer. There's too much work to do. I build the mast out of a couple of two-by-fours glued together—even shape it with a hand plane and sandpaper until it's nicely rounded. Well, round-ish. I build the yard, a long spar to hang the lateen sail from. I build a mast step and mast partner. I install cleats: halyard cleats, yard cleats, leeboard cleats, lots of cleats.

Back at my brother's house the next weekend, I stand around watching while he turns a twenty-dollar plastic tarp and a roll of carpet tape into something more like a sail. Then home again, where I build the leeboards, big pear-shaped slabs of plywood tied onto the sides of the hull like retractable fins so that, in theory, the boat should be able to move forward against the wind rather than just sliding sideways.

But wood floats, and the leeboards will have to sink to work. I cut a circular hole in each board big enough to hold about ten pounds of lead, then buy a bucket of old wheel weights from a tire store and fire up my little single-burner backpacking stove. I throw a bunch of the weights in an old pot and set it on the burner, trying to hold my breath and avoid touching anything, hoping there's no moisture in the pot to make the molten metal spatter explosively. It's a legitimately dangerous operation. I should be wearing leather gauntlets, a heavy apron, a face shield. Instead I'm wearing jeans and a sweatshirt, holding my breath, and trying to stand upwind of everything. Lead, I know, is toxic.

It's also incredibly heavy—too heavy for my stove, it turns out. The entire set-up is tilting, the pot slumping sideways as the burner collapses beneath it.

"You probably should have used a bigger stove," the boat says, watching my backyard foundry crumple and spill long dribbles of molten metal across the driveway. I'm too busy pouring what's left of the lead from the pot into the leeboard holes to answer. There's not enough to fill them. I throw a few more chunks of lead in the pot and set it back on the mangled burner for a few minutes, then try another pour. No good. The new lead refuses to mingle with the old.

"Assimilate!" I shout at the lead, poking it with a long-handled spoon. "Stop clinging to your own separate identities so selfishly and defer to the greater good. Unity! We must have unity!"

But it's no good. The new lead stays shiny and new and entirely separate from the old lead. I wait a few hours for everything to cool down and then pry off the new lead, which has formed thin disks on top of the old lead without sticking to it. I throw the shiny disks of new lead into a corner of the shed and stare at the leeboards with their half-filled circles. I'll have to remove the first pour and try all over.

I tap the lead circle with a hammer: a dull thud. I hit harder. Nothing. I pound. Still nothing. I go looking for a bigger hammer. I thump. I pound. I jump up and down on the lead. Nothing. I jump harder. The little circles of lead stay firmly stuck to the leeboards. I pound and jump and pound some more. The half-inch plywood bends and cracks until each leeboard takes on a gentle curve, like a giant palm leaf gently curling in the sun. The lead stays firmly fixed.

Days go by. Finally I buy another sheet of plywood and make new leeboards, melt and pour more lead. Install some cheap half-round molding strips for rubrails. Build a rudder and tiller. And so it goes. Finally there are no pieces left to add. Nothing else to buy, no more supplies to gather. It's time to paint.

"How about a nice bright blue?" Jagular suggests. "Something cheery and tropical."

"A Pirate Racer is like a Model T," I tell him. "You can have any color you want as long as it's black. Now don't bother me. We're launching tomorrow and I want to get at least two coats of paint on."

"We're launching tomorrow?" the boat says.

"Yep," I say, dipping my roller into the tray to reload. "We're meeting my brother at Bear Lake. And you know how anytime two boats are sailing together, it's a race? Well, my brother's boat is twelve feet long, you're fourteen and a half. And in sailing, length equals speed. We've got an extra twenty-five square feet of sail besides—we'll be sure to win."

"Uh-huh," Jagular says. "Isn't that a water-based latex paint you're using?"

I pick up the can to read the label. "That's what it says here," I tell him. "Why?"

A moment goes by before the boat answers. "Never mind," he says.

◆   ◆   ◆

Bear Lake is a long weed-fringed pond with a wide spot in the middle where power boaters circle around a couple of buoys, pulling little kids on inner tubes. Now and then one of them falls off and starts to cry. The obnoxious two-stroke buzz of outboard motors fills the air, along with the smell of gasoline. The sun beats down on everything relentlessly.

There's a boat ramp somewhere but not at this side of the lake where the campground is, so my brother and I back our trailers through the pines as close to the water's edge as we can. From there we carry our boats down to the beach one by one and lay them on the sand side by side, ready for launching.

My brother has designed his own boat instead of building from plans, and I can't help thinking that the result is better than it should have been. Like my boat, it's a simple flat-bottomed skiff. But where Jagular has a boxy slab-sided hull, my brother chose to fit three overlapping plywood planks on each side, a method that seems elegant and old-fashioned in comparison. Then instead of painting, he oiled the bare wood. Whenever people see his boat they say things like "Is that an antique?" and "Did you build that yourself?"

When they see Jagular they hurry past without saying anything.

But neither boat has been in the water yet—today's the day. After messing around for an hour or so with all the fussy little bits of ropes and rigging that should've been done before we got here, figuring out where to tie this and how to attach that, we finally get things mostly settled and pull both boats off the beach into the water. My brother steps his mast and raises the boat's spritsail, hops in, pulls the sheet taut, and sails away. Jagular floats free in the ankle-deep water, ready to follow.

"Somehow I thought there'd be a little more excitement," I tell him.

"Just wait," Jagular says.

Standing in the shallows beside him, I take the halyard in hand to hoist the sail for the first time. It's a lot bigger in person than it was in the plans, this lateen rig—an eighty-five-square-foot triangle hanging from the yard, an eighteen-foot-long wooden club that runs along the top edge of the sail. The rig is heavy and cumbersome and seems ridiculously oversized. The yard is longer than the entire boat, in fact, which makes it incredibly awkward to handle. It overhangs the boat on both ends getting in the way of everything else while the sail billows around filling up the cockpit and spilling out into the water.

"Here goes," I say, and start to pull on the halyard. The yard slides reluctantly up the mast, unbalanced and spinning around uncontrollably, swinging at my shoulders and head.

The sail tries to wrap itself around everything as it rises with the yard. The boat rocks back and forth violently under the yard's shifting weight.

"See what I mean?" Jagular says.

"Shut up," I tell him, and duck another clobbering from the yard. One hand for the halyard and one for the yard, that's what it takes. And one hand to guard your head and various other appendages. But finally I get the sail up and the halyard cleated off, leaving the whole rig hanging free above the cockpit. We're ready to set sail. Stepping carefully into the middle of the cockpit, I sit down with my back against the side deck, tiller in hand.

"We're off," I say.

But the boat doesn't move. The leeboards are aground, I realize, digging deeply into the sandy bottom and holding us stuck fast to the beach. I raise the boards and tie them off to their cleats.

"Ok," I tell the boat. "Now we're off. Get going."

There's not much wind, though, and it's almost too hot to be out here without it. Even the power boaters have given up; everything has wound down, all momentum drained from the day. But we slowly move away from the beach neverthe-less, out toward deeper water. Motion without energy, accel-eration without effort. It's incredibly satisfying, if not terribly exciting. Even in this dead calm there's enough wind to keep the sails filled. We're sailing.

◆   ◆   ◆

"You know, I could swim faster than this," I tell Jagular after a few minutes. "I thought you were a Pirate *Racer*."

"It's not my fault," the boat says. "You must have done something wrong when you were building me."

We drift along for a few minutes more without saying any-thing else, and after a while we're closer to the opposite shore than to our launching point. Still not much wind. Overhead the sail waves slowly back and forth without enthusiasm. The water is flat and motionless. The occasional bass or bluegill flickers past beneath us looking for shade. A horsefly buzzes slowly around my head, too lazy to attack.

Up ahead my brother's boat has reached the far end of the lake and is heading back.

"Day after day, day after day, we stuck, nor breath nor motion," I say, trailing my fingers in the water and flicking them at the horsefly, which lands on the side deck and eyes me suspiciously. We slide a few yards farther across the lake. Still too hot. Now and then the shadow of the sail falls across the cockpit and brings a moment of shade.

Exciting stuff, this sailing.

The horsefly eventually abandons ship and takes off on a sluggish flight across the lake, back toward the distant campground. Meanwhile we're ghosting along toward the opposite shore. Nothing ahead of us but swampy low land and, a few yards back, an overgrown woodland thick with brambles and deerflies.

We drift for a few more minutes, getting slowly closer to the swamp and the waiting woods. Emphasis on the slowly. There's plenty of time to practice: I experiment with the leeboards, raising and lowering them, tying and untying lines, making changes and adjustments as if I know what I'm doing. I experiment with the mainsheet, pulling the line in tighter, letting it run free, dropping it overboard, retrieving it. I shift my weight forward. I shift back. I move to the leeward side of the boat. I sit on the side deck. None of it makes any difference. We're still drifting along at sub-glacial speeds, approaching the tall reeds and cattails at the lake's edge.

We're about to be sliding right into the weeds, actually— we've been moving so slowly that I haven't been paying much attention. I push the tiller back and forth in a couple of last-

Still not much wind.

minute attempts at evasive action, but we're not moving fast enough for the rudder to steer us.

"Probably would've been a good idea to bring some oars along," Jagular says.

Then the bow pushes past the first row of cattails and we slide past into the swamp. Everything is quiet except for the sound of marsh grass and cattails scraping the hull as we keep drifting forward. Soon all but a thin swath of the lake is out of sight behind us. We're following a narrow channel, a slim reedy passage barely wider than Jagular's hull, a tunnel leading deep into the weeds and lily pads and dark still waters of the marsh. A one-way dead-end passage.

"Yep," the boat says. "Oars. For rowing and stuff, don't you think?"

Far across the lake behind us, my brother sails past our narrow window, his boat gliding smoothly and silently across the deep water, its jaunty spritsail catching the sunlight with a flash of white. A few faint waves ripple across the surface of the water behind him, the first stirrings of an approaching wind.

Here in the weeds the air is thick and still. With a dull *shluuuck* we nose into the mud, aground. A few seconds later the horsefly reappears, buzzing in slow circles above my head, dropping lower and lower with each pass until it, too, finally comes to rest. It eyes me from the foredeck, safely out of reach.

◆   ◆   ◆

"Yep," Jagular says as I'm tying everything onto the trailer for the drive home. "The longer boat is the faster boat."

"Speed isn't everything."

"And paint's peeling off the bottom of the hull in sheets, you know," he goes on, paying no attention to my interruption.

It's true; large swaths of paint litter the ground beneath the trailer, rubbery black sheets like pieces of coated paper. I pick one up—thin and slimy. Slightly stretchy.

"All right, maybe I should have let the paint dry a little longer," I say. "But the fiberglass makes the hull completely waterproof anyway. The paint is purely cosmetic."

"Most impressive, though," Jagular goes on, still ignoring me—"most impressive was the way you sailed us so far into those weeds that we had to have your brother come back and tow us out."

"I can't help it if you refuse to sail backwards," I say.

I'm not really paying much attention to the conversation, though, because I'm trying to figure out how to tie an eighteen-foot spar onto a fourteen-foot boat. I've run out of straps. All I have left is the mainsheet, which I wrap around and around everything I can reach until the entire cockpit is filled with a web of lines. Finally I decide it's good enough, climb into the car, and drive off. Jagular bumps along on the trailer behind me, chuckling quietly. I glance in the rearview mirror as we reach the campground exit, and I can see long shreds of black paint hanging from the bottom of the hull.

"Well," I tell the boat. "Nobody's perfect."

"That's for sure," he says.

Just as we're about to pull onto the highway, a horsefly buzzes in through the window and lands on the dash in front of me. He looks up at me briefly, glances back at Jagular, then shakes his head and flies away.

Jagular in the North Woods

S OME WEEKS LATER—never mind how long precisely— having little or no money in my purse, and nothing particular to interest me on shore, I thought I would sail about a little and see the watery part of the world.

"I see you've been to the library again," Jagular says.

"Nonsense," I tell him. "I'm done with all that for now. It's time to go off into the world and see what there is to be seen, do what there is to be done. It is a way I have of driving off the spleen, and regulating the circulation."

"What does that even mean?"

I stop for a moment and look around. The lawn needs another mowing. The door to the carriage house or garage or whatever it is has fallen off again. The walls are buckling and the whole structure is sinking slowly into the ground. The house isn't much better. Roof. Windows. Furnace. Floors. Everything falling into ruin.

"It means Thoreau was right when he wrote that the trappings of domesticity are more easily acquired than got rid of," I say. "So, with a philosophical flourish Cato throws himself upon his sword; I quietly take to the ship."

"You might be better off throwing yourself on your sword," the boat says.

I ignore him. "Now, when I say that I am in the habit of going to sea whenever I begin to grow hazy about the eyes, and begin to be over conscious of my lungs, I do not mean to have it inferred that I ever go to sea as a passenger. For to go as a passenger you must needs have a purse, and a purse is but a rag unless you have something in it.

"Besides, passengers get sea-sick—grow quarrelsome—don't sleep of nights—do not enjoy themselves much, as a general thing;—No, I never go as a passenger; nor, though I am something of a salt, do I ever go to sea as a Commodore, or a Captain, or a Cook."

"Mainly because you'd actually have to cook something instead of just eating cold ravioli from a can," the boat says.

"More nonsense," I say. "No, I abandon the glory and distinction of such offices to those who like them. For my part, I abominate all honorable respectable toils, trials, and tribulations of every kind whatsoever. It is quite as much as I can do to take care of myself, without taking care of ships, barques, brigs, schooners, and what not."

"That's true enough," Jagular says.

"Now cease your foolish badgering," I tell the boat. "For there is a place not far from here," I say, "a watery web of lakes and islands and swamps, a hidden wilderness at the very headwaters of the Chippewa River. It is a place unlike any other, replete with virgin timber and clear fast-running streams, a place where we shall see bears and wolves, and mooses, and minks, and otters; we shall discover muskellunges and snapping turtles of the largest size. Deers and coyotes and perhaps even ocelots roam the forests; red-eyed loons make the waters echo with their eerie calls; eagles swoop low over the rushing waters, and wood ducks gather in flocks so large that they blacken the very skies with their passing."

"Why are you telling me all this again?" Jagular says. "It's all you've been talking about for weeks now. And besides, I doubt we'll be seeing any ocelots."

"Who knows what we shall discover?" I say. "For we shall be alone in the north woods—"

"I thought your brother was meeting us there."

"He is. But we'll be alone anyway. His boat is faster in light airs, but if we get any real wind we'll leave him behind." I stop for a moment to gather my thoughts. "So. We shall be alone in the north woods, free to find whatever is waiting to be found; we shall roam the waters at will and camp where we please, moving from one island to the next, riding the wind where we can, and rowing where we must."

Silence.

"You may want to think this over a little more," the boat suggests finally. "Just for example, can I ask how you plan to stow an eighteen-foot yard in a fourteen-foot boat when we have to strike the rig to row?"

"No," I tell him. "You can't."

"What about oarlocks?"

"Over-rated," I say. "But we do have oars this time. I can just bungee them to the leeboard cleats for now."

"How about a real tiller?"

It's a good question. Jagular's tiller is truly pathetic, a hastily chopped off and rounded two-by-two with feeble half-inch tongues screwed on to overlap the rudder cheeks and hold the quarter-inch bolt that secures the tiller to the rudder head. The whole thing is outlandishly crude and over-sized, but constructed so poorly it'll probably fall apart the first time we try to tack. Even I'm ashamed of it, and that takes some doing. No time to fix it, though, so I just aim an angry stare at the boat.

"What about some reef points, then?" Jagular asks. "Eighty-five square feet is an awful lot of sail area."

"Humbug!" I say. "Reefing is for sissies. Sailing is supposed to be exciting, not just sitting around being wet and bored. Fear is an essential ingredient of any adventure, the crucible in which the raw clay is fired, the molten steel tempered."

Jagular sighs. "The paint is still peeling off the bottom, you know."

"I never look at the bottom of the boat while I'm sailing anyway," I say. "Besides, the rig is tied down. The gear's all packed. My wife isn't looking. Let's go."

◆   ◆   ◆

Several hours later we arrive at the headwaters, a quiet collection of lakes and streams surrounded by a second-growth forest of pine, birch, oak, and maple. It's late afternoon, and the unpaved parking lot is empty. The real north woods—endless tracts of white pines two hundred feet tall, trees so big that two or even three men together couldn't reach around them—those north woods are gone forever, I know, the trees clear-cut and stacked up and hauled out and rafted down to riverside sawmills in Eau Claire and Chippewa Falls and a hundred other lumber towns that have faded into obscurity, the forest not endless after all. But at least it's not the bleak fields of amputated stumps we would have found a hundred years ago—it's not the north woods of frontier mythology, exactly, but it's better than I'd hoped for. Wind ruffling the leaves overhead, the play of dappled sunlight and shifting shadows, long stretches of undeveloped woodland, and an intricate weaving of interconnected lakes, real northwoods lakes with clean dark tannin-infused water and shorelines bristling with birches and pines.

After unloading the trailer and leaving Jagular on a sandy beach beside the boat ramp, I park the car at the edge of the lot and come back for a look around. There's a Department of Natural Resources bulletin board and a box full of brochures with a map of the flowage on one side. I take one and walk down to the water's edge.

Before long, my brother's Jeep rattles into the parking lot. He unloads his boat, and we take a brief look at the map together, somehow avoiding any agreements or decisions—our usual approach to planning. Then I launch Jagular and set off, steering a broad reach north past Scott Island and Turkey Vulture Island and a half dozen other islands scattered across the map, too small for names. A quarter mile behind us my brother launches his boat and follows in our wake.

◆   ◆   ◆

Just past Turkey Vulture Island the wind dies away to nothing, leaving us floating around listlessly. I start to fiddle with the sheet and leeboards, trying to find a combination that will give us maximum drive and minimum drag. Nothing seems to make any difference.

"The vultures are going to get us at this rate," Jagular says.

"You be quiet," I tell him.

My brother finally catches up, and we drift around side by side for a while. The map on the free DNR brochure isn't exactly matching what we see around us, which disturbs him immensely. He keeps looking down at the map, then looking up at the islands. There's a large island just south of us. But the map shows a medium-sized island, a stretch of open water, and two tiny islands. He knows perfectly well where we are—if I know, he surely knows—but he insists on things being right. Disorder, ineptitude, things done poorly—for my brother these are wrongs that must be righted, no matter the cost.

"Why worry about it? That has to be Turkey Vulture Island," I tell him. "We sailed north from the boat ramp and then turned west. It's the only thing that makes sense."

"Turkey Vulture Island's not shaped like that on the map," he insists.

"Look, Big Banana Island is right there," I point out. "And that's Little Banana, with the channel between them. We can't be anywhere else."

But order must be restored, the errant stars set back in their courses, and my brother knows I won't be the one to do it. He keeps staring at the map as if trying to force it to match our surroundings by sheer force of will. I'm getting tired just watching him. It's a lot easier to be me than it would be to be anyone else, I decide.

"It can't be that easy," Jagular says. "So far you're the only one who has managed it."

I choose to take it as a compliment.

◆   ◆   ◆

According to the now-suspect map, there's a campsite about a mile ahead on Pine Island, just where the channel between Big Banana Island and Little Banana Island opens up again. When my brother finally gives up on figuring things out, we decide to camp there for the night. We drift around some more, working our way into the narrow passage between the two islands. Sometimes we're closer to one. Sometimes we're closer to the other.

All around us the water stays flat and smooth. The air stays still and silent. The sun drops slowly toward the horizon. Nothing else seems to be moving. There's a bald eagle circling overhead but even he seems motionless, painted onto the evening sky.

I pull up the leeboards entirely to reduce friction with the water, try poling the sail out with an oar to catch what little wind there might be. We creep forward.

My brother drops his sail and starts rowing. He draws even, then passes us.

I pull out our oars.

"I bet you're wishing you had some oarlocks," Jagular says.

"Nonsense," I say. "Watch this." I pull a mass of bungee cords from the stowage compartment in the bow and start to lash one oar to the starboard leeboard cleat. But it's not going to work—the leeboard is in the way.

"I'm watching," Jagular says.

I'll have to untie the leeboard and stow it in the cockpit if I want to row. Both leeboards, I realize. Lead-weighted slabs the size of coffee tables. The hell with that, I decide. We can ghost in, even if it takes a little longer.

Meanwhile my brother's boat is moving steadily down the channel toward Pine Island. He pulls gently at the oars. His boat glides forward. He looks around at the sky. The soaring eagle. The lake. The trees. He pulls at the oars again, putting so little effort into the stroke that I can barely see him move. He looks around again: lake, sky, trees, eagle. Takes another half stroke with the oars. The gap between us is growing steadily.

"Still watching," Jagular says.

Grumbling and muttering, I pull the leeboards aboard and try to find someplace to put them where they're not entirely in the way. I lash the oars to the leeboard cleats, securing each one with an ugly overlapping tangle of bungee cords, trying to create enough tension to hold the oars in place. Then I raise the kick-up rudder and lash the tiller amidships. All the while the sail swings back and forth above the cockpit on its eighteen-foot spar. Nowhere to go with that. It'll have to stay hoisted. I lash the sail into an untidy bundle with some bits of line. Even with the sail furled and mostly out of the way, the weight of the yard makes the boat rock back and forth alarmingly each time I shift my weight.

Up ahead my brother unfurls his spritsail and stows his oars. He's clear of the wind shadow of Little Banana Island now, out in the open where there's some breeze again, sailing slowly toward the sandy spit at the tip of Pine Island.

Finally I'm ready to row. There's no seat aboard Jagular, so I stack a couple of float cushions under me so I can reach the oars comfortably. With bungee cords for oarlocks I can't put much force into my stroke or the oars will pop right off the leeboard cleats, but it's working, kind of. We're moving.

My brother's boat glides up onto the sand spit and he steps lightly ashore.

Aboard Jagular, the exposed bolt heads on the leeboard cleats are grinding away at the oars with every stroke. The float cushions I'm sitting on shift and slide around underneath me as I pull and I have to stop every few strokes to adjust them. The sail unfurls itself and spills into the cockpit until finally I stop rowing to retie it.

Rowing again, but the bungees are stretching. After a while the starboard oar pops off the cleat entirely. I re-tie it. Two strokes later the port oar pops off. I re-tie it.

"Oarlocks," the boat muses quietly.

"Shut up," I say.

Meanwhile my brother has returned from his exploration of Pine Island and starts to unload camping gear from his boat.

I adjust the cushions and take another stroke. The cushions slide apart beneath me, spilling me onto the cockpit floor. Both oars pop off their bungees simultaneously, and Jagular drifts to a halt in the shallows just off Big Banana Island.

"The hell with this," I tell the boat. "We're sailing in from here."

"Want to bet?" Jagular says, but I pretend not to hear.

I unwrap the bungees and the oars, tie the leeboards back onto the boat, and unfurl the sail. I untie the tiller and lower the rudder, adjust the cushions, then sit back down. The tiller is lifeless in my hand. The sail waves back and forth without ambition. If I try hard enough, though, I can almost imagine some faint motion toward Pine Island where my brother is sitting alone on the beach now, leaning comfortably against a huge log, his boat and gear safely stowed for the night.

Off to the west behind the islands, the sun drops below the treetops. The sky grows slowly darker. Stars are appearing in the twilight, first one, then another. And another. Whole constellations eventually. The Big Dipper. Cassiopeia. And, faint at first but growing steadily brighter, the Little Dipper. The North Star.

"At least we're not going to get lost," Jagular says.

Ahead on Pine Island my brother calmly gathers firewood, lights a fire. The cheery flicker of the flames is mirrored in the dark water, a shining path lighting our way to camp. Somewhere off across the water a loon calls. The sail hangs overhead without doing anything at all. We keep not moving slowly toward the shore.

◆   ◆   ◆

Next morning we're up early for a sail westward into Chicago Bay, then back to Pine Island for breakfast. After that we're off again, sailing away northward into the remotest stretches of the lake system. There's enough wind that Jagular and my brother's boat seem to be evenly matched today. In fact, we're actually pulling ahead. I'm relieved that we're doing so well for a change, but carefully avoid mentioning it lest such hubris invite a smiting.

We continue farther into the maze of islands, stopping here and there to explore, until we pass through Minnesota Bay and round a corner into a sudden southeasterly wind that's hammering up a narrow channel, funneling itself between the trees like a torrent from a high-pressure hose. And of course we've reached the northwestern edge of the lake, with nowhere to go but southeast, directly into the wind. Large trees are creaking and shifting overhead and branches are breaking off and we can barely manage to hold a beam reach across the channel. We pull into an empty DNR campsite at the north edge of the channel for lunch, but even ashore the wind is fierce. There's no getting around it. We're going to have a tough beat back to Pine Island.

"We could always just go back the way we came and avoid these headwinds entirely," Jagular points out.

"Faint heart ne'er won fair maid," I tell him. "Fortune favors the bold."

And besides, my brother has already launched his boat and is tacking steadily down the channel ahead of us. Steadily, but very slowly. I shove Jagular back into the water—the tall lateen rig gets tangled in the trees overhead until I carefully work it free—and we're off on a port tack, heading south across the channel. We'll have to short tack our way down this narrow passage for a mile, right into the teeth of the wind. Then at last we'll reach open water where we can turn south toward camp.

"Here goes," I tell the boat as we approach the southern shoreline. "Tacking!"

But no.

"Tacking!" I say, trying again. Still not. But there's no way we can survive a gybe in this wind so we don't have any other options.

"Tacking!" I say, louder this time, shoving the crude tiller to leeward, feeling it flex dangerously in my hand. And then the tall sail is tangled in the trees and branches are scraping along the mast and other branches are breaking off and falling on my head and we're aground. The bow slides up onto the island at the southern edge of the channel. I jump out into knee-deep water and start pulling the boat out of the trees.

"Is that what they mean by cursing like a sailor?" Jagular asks.

I'm too busy to answer, trying to get the boat pulled around into the wind to untangle the sail and manage the sheet and reset the leeboards for a starboard tack. Then I jump in and we're heading back north across the channel. The narrow channel.

"Tacking!" I say. "Tacking!"

And then the rig is in the trees and the boat is aground and we're back on the northern shore. We've made about a boat length's worth of progress to windward. I jump back into the water, drag the boat around, and re-launch on the port tack.

"Tacking!" I say.

"I'll say this for you," Jagular says. "You don't give up easily."

And then the rig is in the trees and we're ashore again.

"Which probably isn't a compliment in your case," the boat adds as I jump out and pull the boat around again. Another boat length to windward, almost. I reset the leeboards. Back on the starboard tack. I shove off into the channel and hop aboard. Up ahead the trees are waiting, waving wildly in the wind as if wanting to be sure we don't miss them.

"Tacking!" I say. "Tacking!"

Meanwhile my brother has calmly sailed his boat through a series of short tacks to the far end of the channel, where he turns south and disappears around a corner. And then the leeboards are scraping the sandy bottom and the sail is in the trees and we're aground again.

✦   ✦   ✦

Our endless beat back to Pine Island last night, tedious as it was, has only made me want more. Sailing through fog-shrouded mornings where islands appear out of the mist like passing ships. Rowing through star-studded moonless nights alive with red-eyed loons and great horned owls. Exploring the maze of islands and channels without regard for times and schedules and routines. Moving quietly through the world by sail and oar, in a boat too small to allow any mental distance from where I am, or what I'm doing.

But instead we're stuck ashore again, pinned down by winds too strong to fight our way past. The morning started out fine, all misty islands and red-eyed loons, but we've spent the last few hours bashing our way to windward across a long stretch of open water, with Jagular thumping through the sharp chop and me hiking out on the side decks, expecting to be flattened by a gust at any moment. Expecting the tiller to snap off in my hands. Expecting something without knowing exactly what. We've never sailed in winds like we've encountered these last few days. And we're not sailing now, either. My brother has continued on out of sight up ahead somewhere, but we haven't been able to tack our way through the narrow channel he passed through to get there. Wherever there is.

"We didn't even manage to reach the channel, actually," Jagular says.

"It's not my fault you won't sail to windward," I tell him. No reply.

"All right," I say finally, "it probably is my fault. But either way, we're stuck here for now."

We've taken refuge on a lonely island at the southern edge of a swampy backwater bay, half a mile from where we last saw my brother. The wind has backed to the south now, twisting and shifting unpredictably through the narrow channels between the islands, bringing headwinds from every direction at once. Anywhere we go from here, we'll be launching from a lee shore. And we'd be lucky to make a beam reach in this wind, which would put us back into the open water if we head west; the swamp, if we head east.

"If we had oarlocks instead of bungee cords, we could just row across the bay and through that narrow bit," Jagular says. "That's how your brother made it."

"But we don't have oarlocks," I tell him. "We're going to have to sail our way out of here if we're getting out at all. And forget about heading west—it's way too windy for us out on the open water with this ridiculous lateen rig. It's a lot worse than it was this morning. There'd be no way to drop the sail without killing myself if things went wrong. Sometimes the smart thing is to wait for things to die down a bit."

There's a long silence.

"We're not going to do the smart thing, are we?" the boat asks.

"Maybe not," I admit. "If we launch on a starboard tack, heading east along the shore all the way up into the head of the bay, we might be able to make the channel on a close reach once we're back on the port tack heading west."

"We haven't managed a close reach since the day before yesterday," Jagular reminds me.

"True. But the worst that'll happen if we don't make it is that we'll wash up in the swamp. That would hardly be the end of the world."

"It might be," Jagular says. "You don't know what's in that swamp."

I stare out at the bay, the violently wind-streaked water, the wildly swaying trees on the opposite shore. Then at the swamp to the east.

"The hell with it," I say, taking a last look at the yard swinging crazily from the top of the mast, the big sail snapping and flogging. "Fortune favors the bold." Then I shove the boat into the water and pull it as far westward along the beach as I can get. If we don't lose too much ground when we tack, we might make it.

◆   ◆   ◆

We don't make it. The wind is so strong now that we can't even manage to tack at all. Each time we try, we shudder to a halt and then fall back onto a starboard tack, heading east-ward into the muddy swamp. I'd drop the rig and row but I can't rig the bungee cords without removing the leeboards, which would take far too long. We'd be ashore before I could manage a single stroke of the oars. Besides, I'd be hammered senseless by the yard as soon as I uncleated the halyard. I could try to turn downwind and run back to the island but I'd probably gybe us and that would really be the end of it.

With each failed attempt at tacking, the wind shoves us farther and farther eastward until finally we're aground in the mud of the swamp with nowhere else to go. I have to let the sheet fly free or the wind is going to capsize us into the muck. Suddenly everything is chaos. The yard is swinging wildly from the top of the mast. The sheet is snapping and back and forth across the cockpit. And there's no way to escape the horrible stench we've sailed into, a cadaverous odor of rot and decay so powerful I can barely keep from vomiting.

"If you're going to puke," Jagular says, "make sure you lean way out over the side."

The sail is flogging madly overhead, the yard swinging around viciously until I'm afraid its weight alone will spill us into the mud. I'll have to do something about the mess before things start to go very wrong, but I can barely think past the urge to vomit. With a sudden lurch I scramble for the side deck.

False alarm. But still the smell surrounds me, the smell of things dead and rotting, a putrid unholy smell far worse than any odor I've ever imagined a swamp could contain. Another series of dry heaves wracks my guts, and again I scramble toward the side deck. Another false alarm.

"I figured out why you're puking," Jagular tells me as I grab hold of the yard, trying to calm things down a bit.

"Why's that?" I ask, barely able to keep from retching again as another wave of putrid stench washes over me.

"Take a look off the starboard bow," the boat says.

I do. There's something—a dead dog, maybe, although it's hard to tell—something floating in the weeds a few feet away, bloated and hairless and obscene and tragic all at once.

"The hell with this!" I say, retching again. Holding my breath, I uncleat the halyard and drop the rig into the swamp. Somehow I don't get clobbered as it falls. Then I pull the whole mess aboard, unfasten the leeboards, throw them into the cockpit, and rig the oars. I use a bit of line to roll up the sail and lash the eighteen-foot yard to the mast above my head, and tie the other end of it to the rudder. There's enough headroom now to row. Barely.

"We still don't have oarlocks," Jagular says.

True. But I'm hoping that dropping the yard and furling the sail has reduced our windage enough that we can make some progress. I start rowing carefully westward across the bay, trying to hug the windward shore where it's a little calmer, pulling as lightly as I can to avoid stressing the bungees. It seems to be working for now. We're making our way slowly out of the swamp, out toward the narrow channel to the north, our only escape route. We might make it this time.

◆   ◆   ◆

"Well, we gave it a good try," Jagular says as the oars pop off the leeboard cleats again. After all the effort we still can't manage enough power to row dead upwind through the channel. The stretched-out bungees can't hold the oars in place. We're going to be pushed back. At least we've made it far enough to avoid Dead Dog Bog this time, though. That's worth something.

Once we're safely ashore on our island again, I wander up and down the tiny beach and wonder what my brother is doing, how far ahead he is. He could be having his own problems with this wind, I realize. His boat is smaller, after all, with less freeboard. No flotation. Less seaworthy than Jagular overall. If he's capsized somewhere in a big gust he might be in real trouble. And there's nothing I can do to help from here.

"There's nothing you could do even if you were with him," Jagular says. "You can't even save us."

I try to come up with some kind of response but he's right. We're stuck. If my brother's in trouble, he's on his own. No one can save him now but himself. And then I see him, rowing calmly back through the channel and across the bay, mast down and sail neatly stowed. The wind pushes him along easily, with just a gentle stroke of the oars now and then. Soon he's stepping ashore and pulling his boat up onto the beach beside Jagular.

I explain what happened, how I can't manage to row anywhere in this wind with my bungee cord oarlocks, and can't make any windward progress under sail. And worse, the narrow channels are funneling the wind in all kinds of conflicting directions, creating headwinds that can't be avoided no matter how often we try to change direction. Still, there's nothing to do but try again. We set out once more from the island, rowing north across the bay. And again, no. It's too windy to row through the final channel. We'd make it with oarlocks. Bungee cords aren't going to do it.

I'm about to give up when my brother suggests a tow. I tie a line to Jagular's mast and toss the other end to him. He cleats it off and starts to row up the narrow channel, dead into the wind, and with both of us rowing we're able to finally make it through the last stretch. We've escaped from Dead Dog Bog. A little farther on we beach the boats again to wait for the wind to die down.

My brother doesn't say anything about the tow but I suspect he's pleased. A wrong has been righted. Order restored. Ineptitude amended by competence.

*With both of us rowing we're able to
finally make it through the last stretch.*

"For now," Jagular says.

◆   ◆   ◆

By evening the wind dies down enough that we're ready to sail. There's a campsite just up ahead, on the east side of Turkey Vulture Island—which still doesn't match the map. We're sailing past a grove of tall dark pines spread across an island that shouldn't be there at all. I puzzle over it for a few moments before giving up and flipping the map over to read the back side as we sail along.

The back side, it turns out, is a DNR pamphlet. It's divided into sections. There's CAMPING. MANAGEMENT. WILDLIFE. THE FISHERY. And BOATING, with a little clip art icon of a bass boat on wavy blue water. I start with BOATING:

The Chippewa Flowage has an abundance of sand and rock bars, stumps, floating bogs and floating driftwood, the pamphlet tells me. *These features are not shown on the map provided and it should not be used for navigation.*

"Oops," I tell the boat. "We've been navigating when we weren't supposed to."

But at least I've found the answer to the mysterious uncharted islands we've been seeing: they're floating bogs. Huge mats of vegetation that form virtual islands adrift on the lake, at the mercy of the wind—here today, there tomorrow. Some of them, I read, have held together for so long that they are covered with forty-foot trees. That's what has thrown us off these last few days. I look closely at the island just off our starboard bow and through the dark water I can see that the whole thing is floating on an immense tangle of tree roots, branches, and driftwood. There'd be room to swim right under it to the other side if you could hold your breath for 400 yards.

"Good luck with that," Jagular says.

"No way," I tell him. "I'm not as dumb as I look."

"No," the boat agrees. "I'm not sure that's even theoretically possible."

I don't bother to reply. Soon enough we're out of the wind and into the lee of Turkey Vulture Island—the real thing this time, not its annex of floating bogs. The campsite is just ahead, more tall pines, a nice sandy beach. My brother, as usual, is in the lead. He sails onto the beach and steps ashore while we're still a hundred yards out.

Aboard Jagular I start to relax, finally. It's been a long day. My eyes are tired from too much sun, my face wind-burned, my hands cramped from holding the sheet and tiller for hours at a time. My body aching from hiking out. My brain worn down from the stress of hours spent expecting disasters that never fully materialized. I'm ready for a fire, a hot drink, a cozy sleeping bag.

"You never bother with campfires," Jagular interrupts. "Or hot drinks. Most nights you don't even take time to light the stove."

"Conserving fuel," I explain.

"Laziness," the boat says.

"Same thing."

"And you don't even have a sleeping bag," Jagular continues, "just a ratty old poncho liner your brother stole from the Army twenty years ago. That's why you always get up so early—you're too cold to keep sleeping. You pretend your early rising reflects hardiness or stoicism or something but really it's just stupidity."

All true. But for now I'm happy to be out of the wind, coasting through a quiet bay, the campsite just fifty yards away. We've done all right today. Mostly. Then I glance around the cockpit and notice I've left the bulkhead hatch open. No big deal here in this sheltered bay, but if we had capsized out in the open water like that, the entire bow chamber would have flooded and who knows if we would ever have gotten out of that mess. I reach down and slide the hatch cover into place, press against it until it's tightly sealed. No need to get too lazy.

And then a sudden gust fills the sail, gybing the heavy yard and heeling the boat dramatically to starboard. I scramble for the port side deck but we're still rolling.

I can hardly believe it, but we're going over, fifty yards from the beach. Everything slows down. There's plenty of time to realize what's happening and no time at all to do anything about it. And then Jagular is on his side and I'm treading water beside him, laughing. The worst has happened and it wasn't very bad at all.

"Pilot error," says Jagular.

"Act of God," I tell him, swimming to the halyard and pulling the mast free. I roll the boat back upright and start to roll the sail up around the yard. Before I get far with my salvage efforts, though, an aluminum fishing boat zips into sight, motoring directly toward us. Two fishermen aboard in flannel shirts, baseball caps and sunglasses. Engine roaring now, speeding up.

"Great," says Jagular. "Two rescues in one day."

"Being towed for twenty yards isn't exactly a rescue," I say.

"Debatable."

"Anyway, there's no way I'm taking a rescue now," I tell the boat. "It's awfully nice of these guys to come rushing over, but we don't need any help."

And then they're here, the driver spinning the boat around and throttling back the motor until the boat slows to a stop behind us, the wake almost capsizing Jagular again.

"Hey!" the driver shouts.

"Here we go," says Jagular.

"I don't—" I start to say, but the boat driver isn't talking to me. He's shouting to my brother, who is sliding his boat back into the water to come see if we need any help.

"Hey!" the driver shouts at him again. "Are you guys camping here tonight?"

"We were planning to," he calls back.

The fishermen look at each other for a moment. Then the driver throttles up the motor and spins the boat around, heading back out into the lake without a word to me. Their wake washes over us again and then we're alone, the drone of the outboard fading slowly as they disappear.

"I'm voting in a new captain," Jagular says. "You can't even get us a rescue."

"I don't see a whole lot of other candidates," I tell him.

"I'll keep looking."

Around us the north woods fade slowly into silence, the last light of the day fading slowly from the sky. It's going to be a beautiful night. Somewhere across the water a loon calls, and another answers. The wind has died down, the skies have cleared. The only sound is the gentle splash of oars as my brother rows out to offer us another tow. I grab the bucket from Jagular's flooded cockpit, climb aboard, and start bailing.

Jagular Gets Rescued

B Y THE TIME WE GET TO THE LAKE, it's pretty windy. I stand with my brother and his five-year-old daughter on the dock looking out at the mess of whitecaps scribbled across the bay, the tall grass along the shore bent double under the rush of wind, the treetops waving wildly. We're on the windward shore, in the lee of the land, and it's still almost too windy to think about going out. But it's late October. This will probably be our last chance to go sailing until spring.

Jagular waits in the water alongside us, big lateen sail flogging violently. The mainsheet whips back and forth through the cockpit trying to wrap itself around the leeboard cleats and oarlocks. The eighteen-foot yard hangs high above at the head of the sail like a gigantic pendulum, a headsman's axe, a Sword of Damocles slung from the masthead. Beneath its weight the boat rocks alarmingly. Behind Jagular, my brother's smaller dinghy bounces and jostles in the waves like a toy.

A fisherman in a baseball cap and sunglasses walks over from where he's been tying his boat down on its trailer. "I don't know if you want to go out there," he says, eyeing our little boats. "It's pretty windy."

I shrug noncommittally and he stomps off muttering, angry at having his advice ignored. "Might as well give it a shot," I tell my brother, and climb down into Jagular's cockpit to untie the bow line. With a good shove we're off the dock and under way. I untangle the sheet and grab the tiller, climbing onto the side deck to hike out. Then I flip the sheet under the leeboard cleat, pull it taut, and we're racing across the bay on a port tack, heading west. West into the wide open water, where we'll find the full force of the wind. I'm vaguely aware that my brother has taken off on a starboard tack instead, heading southeast, hugging the shore closely.

"Don't judge him too harshly for his caution," I tell Jagular. "After all, he has a small child along."

"So do I," the boat mutters.

Grinning, I grip the sheet tighter and pull harder, leaning back to hold the boat upright against the power of the wind. Above me the yard pitches back and forth heavily, throwing us from side to side. Waves are splashing against the hull, spray flying into the cockpit. I laugh out loud and pull the sheet in even tighter, leaving my brother and his little boat far behind.

◆   ◆   ◆

Almost immediately I can tell it's too windy to be out here after all—way too windy. I consider heading back to the dock but we wouldn't be able to make any windward progress anyway. The waves would kill our momentum and leave us in irons if we try to tack. I don't even want to think about gybing with the weight of the yard slamming around overhead. Unable to come up with any reasonable alternatives, I keep us pointed out into the bay instead. The wind grows steadily stronger as we leave the sheltered waters near shore farther and farther behind, the sound of the wind through the treetops growing louder and louder. And then, with a peculiar and completely unhurried inevitability, a sustained gust combines with a series of particularly steep waves that we can't point high enough to take at a favorable angle. As the waves throw us further off balance, the boat rolls over slowly onto its starboard side under the weight of the wind, dumping me over the leeward rail into the middle of the bay, just upwind of a shallow reed bed.

"Well, that didn't take long," Jagular says.

I climb to my feet in the waist-deep water, laughing loudly. Cold, but not too bad. Especially for late October. The wind is still blowing hard, and everything that was in the boat is doing its best to float away—right shoe, seat cushion, flashlight, oars, left shoe—but as far as I can see there's no harm done. My brother and his daughter are watching from their boat a couple of hundred yards away, tucked in behind some trees along the shore. They're safely out of the wind. I point at Jagular floating on his side and shrug elaborately, then turn back to the boat.

"You don't have to be prepared as long as you're willing to suffer the consequences," I tell Jagular, and start grabbing stuff and shoving it back into the cockpit. Meanwhile I'm thinking things through. Flip the boat back upright, bail it out, and sail back. Or maybe row back, I decide, thinking of trying to hoist the sail out here with no dock to stand on and nothing to keep us from drifting quickly into the weeds before we get moving. It's awfully windy.

My analysis is interrupted by the sound of a powerboat racing toward me across the water. It's the fisherman in the baseball cap. He's seen us go over and re-launched his boat to come to our rescue.

"This is going to be good," Jagular says.

"That's what I'm afraid of," I tell the boat, watching the fisherman racing toward us. He spins his boat to a halt right beside us, almost tangling the outboard's prop in the various lines and ropes and bungee cords all floating around Jagular's hull in a tangled mess.

"GET IN THE BOAT!" he shouts dramatically, reaching out a hand to pull me aboard. "CLIMB IN!"

"Uh... no thanks," I tell him.

"YOU WON'T LAST TEN MINUTES IN THIS COLD WATER!" he shouts. "I ALREADY CALLED THE FIRE DEPARTMENT! NOW GET IN THE BOAT!"

I glance back at the dock to see a furious procession of law enforcement officers and medical teams arriving: Police car! Ambulance! Fire truck! County sheriff! Fire truck! County sheriff! Police car! County airboat crew and rescue divers! They're all racing to the ramp, lights flashing, brakes screeching as they pull in. People in various uniforms start to jump out of their cars. They're pointing at us, talking on radios, gesturing urgently in all directions.

I take a quick look around. I'm standing in hip-deep water a hundred yards offshore, waves gently slapping against my thighs. Jagular floats high on his side, an inch or two of water in the cockpit, the big lateen sail billowing across the surface of the water like a blanket. Overhead the sun shines brightly in a cloudless sky.

But the fisherman is still shouting at me from his bass boat. "GET IN THE BOAT RIGHT NOW!" he shouts. "HYPOTHERMIA IS A KILLER!"

On shore, meanwhile, all the police officers and sheriffs and EMTs are running along the docks waving and shouting, and the airboat crew is busily launching their boat in a flurry of energetic commands. Reaching over to Jagular's forward bulkhead, I untie the halyard, pull the mast out of the step, roll up the sail around the spars, and calmly flip the boat upright, stowing the whole bundle aboard.

"GET IN THE BOAT!" the fisherman shouts at me, still holding out his hand to pull me aboard. "COLD WATER IS NO JOKE!"

As usual, Jagular's cockpit is nearly filled with water once I have the boat back upright. But at least I haven't lost the bailer. It's tucked safely away inside the watertight compartment in the bow.

"Too bad you didn't put the access hatch in the deck instead of the bulkhead, though," Jagular says. "That way you could open it now without flooding the watertight compartment."

"You be quiet," I tell the boat. I'm thinking over my options: climb in and row back without bailing? Too much water sloshing around in the cockpit. I'd probably capsize several more times on the way, and have to weather several more rescue attempts.

"GET IN THE BOAT!" the fisherman shouts. "YOUR JUDGMENT IS IMPAIRED!"

"He got that right, at least," Jagular says. I ignore them both.

I could walk back to the dock through the shallow water, I suppose, pulling Jagular behind me. I've almost made up my mind to do it when I hear the airboat buzzing toward us, finally launched and on its way. It's too late to get myself out of this, I realize—the crew is determined to rescue something now that they've gone to all this trouble. They're all leaning eagerly over the sides of their boat to scan the horizon in all directions as they race toward us, shouting orders to each other, readying heaving lines and ring buoys, and gesturing enthusiastically in their bright orange life jackets and their bright orange boat.

"Wait for the airboat crew," I ask Jagular, "or take a tow from the fisherman?"

"Fisherman," Jagular says.

"Fisherman," I agree with a sigh, taking a last look at the rapidly approaching airboat. They're nearly in ring buoy range already.

"GET IN THE BOAT!" the fisherman shouts at me again. "NOW!"

"All right," I tell him, climbing over the side, Jagular's bow line in my hand. The fisherman is so surprised at my sudden

They race toward us, shouting orders to each other, readying heaving lines and ring buoys, and gesturing enthusiastically.

acceptance that for a moment he isn't sure what to do. Then he puts the motor in gear and nudges the throttle, turning us toward the dock. The airboat buzzes to a slow stop in the middle of the bay behind us. The crew slumps in disappointment, the bright orange hull sinking lower in the water as it loses speed.

◆   ◆   ◆

When we arrive at the dock, dozens of policemen and sheriffs and deputies are waiting. They're all stumbling and lunging frantically toward us, getting in each other's way, intent on pulling me safely onto dry land. Meanwhile the ones who don't have room to be directly involved stand on the sidelines shouting at me to report to the ambulance immediately lest I succumb on the spot to hypothermia. They seem surprised that I'm not dead already. I give myself a quick once-over—thin quick-drying nylon pants, wet to the waist but already starting to dry; a bulky wool turtleneck sweater slightly damp around the bottom edge; a warm and mostly dry long underwear shirt underneath—and wonder what danger I'm in, especially now that I'm back on dry land with a change of clothes waiting in my car, only five feet away.

In the middle of my self-assessment, several townspeople rush over from their lakeside homes and try to wrap blankets around me. Behind them two ambulance crewmen are working their way through the crowd, brandishing blood pressure cuffs and thermometers and stethoscopes and IV bags, advising me to submit to medical attention immediately. It's all too much.

"Look," I tell the blanket throwers, "there's no emergency here. I don't need your help." Then I turn to one of the ambulance guys. "Somewhere in your kit you have a form for me to sign to record my utter and complete rejection of medical treatment," I tell him. "Handing me that form and a pen to sign it with is the only assistance I'm going to accept."

They all wander away reluctantly. The ambulance guys are too disappointed to even bother with the paperwork.

Meanwhile, some of the sheriffs and policemen out on the edge of the action give up their attempts at direct involvement in the dramatic rescue and start prowling the docks inspecting everything. I suddenly remember that there's no life jacket aboard Jagular.

Sure enough, one of the cops approaches me. "How come you're not wearing a life jacket?" he asks.

"The water's only waist deep," I point out. He insists that I would have been safer wearing it, and scolds me for my poor judgment. Next, he wants to know where my life jacket is, since I'm not wearing it.

"Uh..." I say. "It must have gone overboard when I flipped." I'm a terrible liar but there's nothing he can do about it unless he wants to re-launch the airboat to go inspect the crime scene for evidence. But I've also just remembered that all boats over twelve feet long have to be registered in Wisconsin, and I'm hoping he doesn't ask about that. He doesn't.

Pretty soon, though, another cop approaches me. They seem to be taking turns, sharing the excitement. "How long is your boat?" this cop asks.

Meanwhile a herd of other sheriffs, cops, and EMTs are still trying to convince me to come to the ambulance—not for medical attention this time, they assure me, but just so I can have some privacy to change clothes. I'm tempted to remind them that the park was empty until they showed up, and that they're the only people I need privacy from, but I doubt they'd be happy to hear it. I've been caught up in a mindless inertia of procedural inevitability, an unthinking cultural force that cannot be resisted but can only be endured. My brother has tied his boat up to the farthest end of the docks where he is watching, I know, with growing amusement. And now, in between fighting off the blanket throwers and the ambulance enthusiasts and wishing I'd been able to get at the bailer instead of taking a tow from the fisherman, I'm eyeing the cop who has just asked me how long my boat is.

Does he have any idea how long a twelve-foot boat is? I ask myself. Probably not; most people don't. Just say twelve feet. He'll never know the difference. But no, I finally decide, better to tell the truth and play dumb if necessary than it would be to lie and watch him whip out a tape measure. I'll be honest. Well, mostly honest, anyway.

"Fourteen feet," I tell him, cutting off half a foot from the actual measurement. The cop nods once and wanders off.

Eventually I manage to push the other sheriffs and cops and airboat guys and EMTs aside so I can get to my car, where I get out my dry clothes and start to change into them. Most of my would-be rescuers finally give up and drive off then, and I pull Jagular up on the ramp to bail. I'm hoping I can get the boat on the trailer and get the hell out of there without having to withstand any more scrutiny when the how-long-is-your-boat cop returns. He seems to derive an unsettling degree of personal satisfaction from informing me that I'm in violation of Wisconsin's boating registration requirements—requirements he's spent the last few minutes looking up when he couldn't think of anything else to do, I suppose.

I feign ignorance, my usual strategy in these kinds of situations. "Oh," I say. "I thought it was boats over sixteen feet long."

"No, it's twelve feet," he tells me.

"Oh," I say. "I didn't know that." Then I keep bailing.

The how-long-is-your-boat cop stands around for a few

moments, clearly hoping for more of a reaction. Then, with a stern admonition about needing to get my boat registered, he finally leaves. The rescue is over.

But no, there's one more sheriff coming, clipboard in hand. He wants to know about the incident. "What happened?" he asks.

"My boat tipped over," I tell him, still bailing.

"How fast were you going at the time of the accident?" he asks, pen poised to take down my answer. "Twenty miles an hour?"

"Uh..." I say, and stop. Twenty miles an hour! He waits, watching me closely.

"You don't know a whole lot about sailing, do you?" I say finally. He shrugs, embarrassed. After a few moments I turn back to the boat and keep bailing. The clipboard sheriff watches for a minute and then finally leaves, probably worrying about how he's going to fill up the blank spaces in his thick pile of paperwork. The park slowly empties until we're left in peace at the boat ramp. Even the fisherman in the baseball cap and sunglasses is gone, and my brother and niece are at the other end of the parking lot tying his boat onto the trailer and getting ready for the drive home.

◆   ◆   ◆

After a long session of bailing and sponging, Jagular is finally dry and clean, the rig neatly stowed away ready for trailering. I back the trailer down the ramp and climb out to pull Jagular out.

"Well," I tell the boat. "I'd say that went remarkably well."

"You're an idiot," Jagular says.

"But it might be time for a new rig. Get rid of that lateen sail with its big heavy yard."

"Maybe not a complete idiot."

"Then we can try something really big next year," I continue. "Like this Texas 200 thing I've been looking into—a five-day cruise along the Gulf of Mexico and the Texas coast. No rules or entry fees. No safety measures or support crews. Remote beaches, high winds, and narrow passes; tricky shoals and blistering sun. Traveling forty miles a day, dodging stingrays and sharks and oyster-shell reefs. No shade. No fresh water. The open sea waiting just beyond the barrier islands, nothing to stop the wind from sweeping in on us like..." I gesture around at the gusty trees, the whitecaps on the bay. "Like this," I say. "Only bigger, and windier. With sharks."

The boat waits quietly as I winch the bow line taut and finish strapping things down.

"I'm thinking maybe a fully battened Chinese junk rig is the way to go," I tell the boat. "Sixty square feet or so. What do you think?"

There's silence for a moment before Jagular answers.

"God help us," he says.

Jagular Goes South

I T'S THE END OF THE SCHOOL YEAR, and as usual, entropy is gaining ground fast. I plod through my last days of teaching, thinking about boat modifications for the Texas 200, a five-day sailing trip along the Texas coast that we've decided to do.

"None of this *we* stuff," Jagular says. "You decided. I'm just getting dragged along to suffer the consequences."

I ignore him. I'm trying to figure out how I'm going to handle a fourteen-foot boat with a nine-foot mast and an eighteen-foot yard in twenty-knot winds, through big salt-water bays with tides and currents and devious oyster-shell reefs and maybe sharks for all I know. I've never done a trip this big before and I'm not sure how stupid it is.

"Pretty stupid if you ask me," Jagular says.

"I didn't," I tell him, and go back to my planning.

I make mental lists of things to do, things to buy. New mast. New sail. New mast step. Through-bolted oarlocks. Paint. An anchor. New tiller. Self-steering. Charts. At the Farm & Fleet, an aisle of folding knives catches my eye. Every sailor needs a knife. What for? Well... they just do. This isn't some little Wisconsin lake, after all. This is the ocean, kind of. Salt spray. Flying fish. Albatrosses. Typhoons. So. Plain knife, or multi-tool? Compromise: a two-piece blade and Phillips screwdriver combo.

Back home, the latest paint job is threatening to peel off

the bottom of the boat again. I pretend not to notice since there's no time to do anything about it. My new Chinese junk sail is a tangled mess of crude battens, duct tape, and strings everywhere. I give up on that and cram the whole mess into a corner of the garage, borrow the spritsail from my brother's boat instead. Tack on new rubrails.

Friday is the last day of school. The students are out early, so I slip home after lunch to pack. The living room has been submerged under piles of gear for days. Now I gather up a couple of bags and backpacks and start to shove everything in. Stove. Gas can. Tent. Raspberry Newtons. Sardines in mustard sauce. Five one-gallon jugs of water. Fork. Run to grocery store. Ramen noodles. Tuna packets. Lemonade mix. Five o'clock. Sleeping bag. Books. Compass. Charts. Five-thirty. Throw a random armload of clean clothes into the back of the car. Throw everything else on top. Hook up trailer. Stop at gas station. Quarter to six Friday night and we're finally on the road.

One-thirty a.m. Sunday morning and we pull into Port Mansfield, Texas. Fred Stone Park, our launching point, turns out to be a clutter of small boats and trailers surrounding a lumpy parking lot of hard-packed dirt, a dock, and a derelict cinderblock building with an overflowing trash barrel, a cold-water sink, and a toilet boldly unencumbered by walls or barriers. Someone has dragged the trash barrel in front of the toilet in an attempt to reduce the exposure.

"Nice to be among civilized people," Jagular says, eying the barrel.

I'm too tired to reply. A yard light at the docks shines into every corner of the parking lot, so I throw my sleeping mat on the dirt in the shadow of the boat and collapse. At least the wind keeps the mosquitoes away.

MONDAY

I wake to the smell of rotting seaweed, which is pretty much how I fell asleep, too. I spent Sunday unloading Jagular and ferrying my car to the finish line at Magnolia Beach, riding a bus back to Fred Stone Park with my fellow sailors. Then I walked up and down the beach in the hot wind looking at all the other boats before collapsing for the night beside Jagular on the sand. For the next five days we'll all be sailing northward along a remote stretch of semi-desert coast, an informal armada of sailors and would-be adventurers. The Texas 200.

Now gray light seeps slowly into the day until I decide there's no point lying here anymore. I stand up, wade through the ankle-deep slime to Jagular, throw my sleeping pad and blanket in, and look around. Texas. There's a kind of gutbucket post-apocalyptic splendor to it, all broad sky and scrub brush. Boats and people are scattered around the beach and anchored offshore, all waiting for the start of this crazy cruise or race or adventure or whatever it is. What look like three or four packing crates are beached nearby—these are the infamous Puddle Ducks, crude plywood dinghies more like sandboxes than boats. Their skippers, an anarchic crowd of rum-swilling hooligans, are strewn around the desolate beach like fresh corpses. Next to me is a Hobie catamaran, beside it a tiny wooden sailboat painted bright blue. There must be thirty or forty boats. If I'm about to do something stupid, I'm not the only one.

"It's windy," I tell Jagular.

"Uh-huh," he says. "Real windy."

I stand there on the beach in the unwavering wind and watch the sun rise slowly above the horizon like an angry red eye. No shade for the next twelve hours. A few more people start moving around. Eventually the Duck skippers stagger down to the beach and drag their boats into thigh-deep water and sail away, and the Texas 200 has officially begun. I stand on the shore trying to think of an excuse not to launch.

"Is your boat going to be all right in this much wind?" someone asks.

"Sure," I say out loud. "Won't be a problem." I have the familiar feeling, though, that despite the reassuring presence of all these other boats and sailors, I am about to do something stupid. The only question is how stupid. The white polytarp spritsail I've borrowed from my brother flaps wildly on the mast as if making a frantic attempt to surrender.

A lean grizzled sailor with white hair and sea-squinty eyes watches my nervous pacing from the beach where he is still calmly building his boat. Last year he was one of the Puddle Duckers. This year he designed himself a flat-bottomed fourteen-footer with two masts, two sails, and a bunch of lines and cleats that he's still figuring out. After a moment he stops what he's doing and gives Jagular a long look.

"You've done a nice job making your sail," he says. "But you might want to tie in a reef before launching." Then goes back to work without waiting to see whether I'll take his advice.

"Your brother made the sail, didn't he?" Jagular asks.

"Shut up," I tell him. I'm trying to figure out what to do about reefing. It's probably a good idea, but there are no reef points in the sail. I never bothered to reef the previous lateen rig either, so I'm not entirely sure how to go about it. But it can't be that hard to figure out. I stare at the flapping sail for a few moments, sure there's a way to set up a reefing system somehow.

"Reef points," Jagular says. "That should've been on your list."

"Too late now," I tell him.

"It usually is," he says.

"The hell with it," I tell Jagular finally. "Let's just go." I could unlace the sail from the mast, roll up the foot, rig some kind of new sheeting point at the clew, re-lace the sail to the mast, and make some kind of crudely reefed sail out of the whole mess, but just thinking about it feels too much like work. Instead I drag Jagular into deeper water, out past the moored boats, and clamber aboard.

It's windy—a steady twenty knots maybe, according to some of the other sailors I've been talking to, who probably don't know any better than I do—and I go through the usual launching fiasco, trying to keep the sheet from snagging on the leeboards, cleats, and tiller, with the boat trying to turn sideways as I fall into the cockpit and sheet in, flopping over the stern to shove down the kick-up rudder, arm soaked to the shoulder, Jagular thumping up and down as I shift my weight, one oar knocked off the oarlock, the sheet wrapped around my ankles, everything happening all at once, until I'm finally away on the starboard tack.

Time to regroup, remind myself that I know what I'm doing. Heading east across the Laguna Madre, the waves are piled up row after row from the south, tossing us around alarmingly as we sail a close reach on a starboard tack. To the north and south the water stretches away as far as I can see, into infinity for all I know, and a wide gray sky hangs down from overhead as if its weight has squashed Texas flat. Far to the east, five or six miles offshore, the long dune-swept finger of Padre Island shelters us from the open Gulf. Still, compared to our usual cruising grounds, this is big water, and big wind. I sail way out past the ICW's line of green and red buoys, nervous about making the turn downwind, when we'll be briefly broadside to the waves. I try a few tentative jabs of the tiller before finally just shoving it over to starboard and holding it there until we're heading north up the Laguna Madre, paralleling the western shore of Padre Island.

A wide gray sky hangs down from overhead
as if its weight has squashed Texas flat.

The Puddle Ducks are way up ahead, then only a long line of ICW buoys stretching into the distance.

◆   ◆   ◆

The wind grows steadily stronger all day, so I'm glad I started as early as I did. After a while I tie off the sheet to the lee-board cleat. You're not supposed to do that, I've read—you want to be able to release the sheet instantly at any moment on a small boat to avoid capsizing in a gust—but the hell with that. My hands are already getting tired and cramping up from holding such a thin line with the weight of the wind pulling against me. If we go over in a gust, we go over.

"*Alea jacta est*," I tell the boat. "If it was good enough for Caesar, who am I to argue?"

After tying off the sheet I fiddle with the self-steering gear, a line and bungee combination tied around the tiller led to jam cleats on the side decks, until it steers the boat better than I can. I'm hands-free. Bailing occasionally. A little scary, but not too bad now that we're out here on our way.

Before long, Jagular starts to surf, a dull roar of wave slipping slowly by underneath. We surge forward on the face of the wave with a flood of exhilaration. Five seconds. Eight seconds. Ten seconds. Then Jagular settles as the wave leaves us behind, starts surfing again on the next wave, and the next. The boat surfs along, steering itself as the bungees tug the tiller back and forth, leaving me in a curious mixture of exhilaration, apprehension, and inactivity. I'd read one of the books I've brought along but it's too wet; each wave sends a stream of water up the starboard leeboard and unto my right shoulder.

One by one I pass the Puddle Ducks, who wave and shout at me as we go by. I wave back and pretend to hear what they're saying. Nice guys. I'm beginning to think their hard-man reputation may have been exaggerated, though. Their boats have back rests. Solar panels. Cabins with actual portholes. Stereos, even! Those Duck skippers look obscenely comfortable, lounging around in their little sandboxes. At least I'm passing them.

But it keeps getting windier, and before long I'm bailing again. Suddenly Jagular gets on top of a big wave and surfs a long time, the longest run yet, then drops off the crest and slams his bow into the wave just ahead. Water pours over the foredeck and into the cockpit, gallons of it. I start bailing frantically, the boat heavy and threatening to broach. I get the cockpit halfway bailed out before Jagular buries his bow again. More water pours into the cockpit, and everything aboard is floating, held in only by tie-down lines. A couple of Raspberry Newtons escape their carton and slide overboard. I finally remember to shift my weight as far back as I can, which holds the bow clear and lets me keep bailing. Eventually the cockpit is back to mostly dry.

The rest of the Laguna Madre passes calmly. I re-open the package of Raspberry Newtons and proclaim the ancient Roman legionary's penalty for desertion: decimation! One out of every ten Newtons must die. I eat four of the remaining thirty-two Newtons.

"Always round up for mutinies and desertions," I explain. No one complains.

Up ahead the Laguna Madre is pinching down to its northern end, and a line of low spoil islands begins off to our right. I stop at one of them to stretch my legs and admire the lack of scenery. Flat sand. Scrub brush. Cactus. Sky. Weeds. Wind. Like sailing past an endless line of abandoned lots.

"You're the one that picked Texas," Jagular reminds me.

"True," I tell him. "But now that I've seen it I'm not sure why. No one in his right mind would come so far for this."

"Exactly," the boat says.

The Ducks have passed us while we've been ashore, so I launch and follow them into the long narrow channel of the Land Cut. From here to tonight's camp we'll be sailing straight down a narrow canal dredged for miles through the mud flats, connecting the Laguna Madre with the bigger bays and channels to the north. Giant wind turbines line the western shore, spinning slowly in the distance as we sail by. Up ahead the Ducks pull in to the eastern shore to regroup, and we pass by without stopping, in the lead now.

"Do you even know where tonight's campsite is?" Jagular asks.

I don't bother to answer.

◆　　　◆　　　◆

It's not long before I'm forced to admit that it's no optical illusion; there's a definite bend to the mast.

"You probably should have built a real mast instead of trying to get by with a left-over steel fence post," Jagular says.

"I built a real mast," I say. "I just decided to use the fence post instead."

"You're an idiot," the boat mutters.

"In theory, the fence post will bend enough to spill the worst gusts, maybe enough to keep us from capsizing," I explain, steering toward the shore for repairs.

"It's bending, anyway," Jagular says. "You got that part right."

I beach us in a mudbank without saying anything else and tug the fence post out of the mast step, then try to straighten it out. There's nothing to pry against, though; the foot of the mast just sinks into the mud. I'm standing knee-deep in gray ooze and have to keep pausing to fight my way out. When I finally get free I try prying the mast against the hull, but the geometry is wrong; the mast rolls across the side decks rather than bending. Meanwhile the rest of the fleet is passing us by, a long string of boats that started later and sailed faster than we did.

"At least we'll know where tonight's campsite is," I say.

"If we manage to get there before dark so we can see them," Jagular grumbles.

But finally I get the mast, if not straightened out, then at least bent a little differently than it was before. I re-step it with the bend to the opposite side, hoping the wind will straighten it. More boats are passing as I launch; we're dropping farther and farther back in the fleet. Time to get moving.

We haven't gone half a mile before the mast is bending again, though. Needs a backstay, I decide. I glance at the anchor line in my gear bucket, the leeboard cleats perfectly located on the side decks. A backstay! I shove the tiller to port, steering for the beach again. But the mast is bending severely now, almost collapsing. I scramble to release the sheet, hoping to stave off complete disaster, but the mast bends farther and farther under the force of the wind, folding sharply at the partner, a right angle bend, until the whole rig lies draped flat across the foredeck, foot still in the step, sail dragging through the water.

Jagular glides gently up onto the shore, burying his bow in the mud again, thirty seconds too late. The sail billows slowly back and forth through the water, waving limply from the now-horizontal mast.

"Well," the boat says, "we're not going to have to worry about gusts anymore. That's the good news."

I hop out without answering, plans already running through my head. Worst case scenario, I ditch the rig entirely and row north up the Land Cut and the ICW to the Padre Island Yacht Club. Can't be more than fifty miles, all downwind. I can camp by myself, I have water for five days, that will be fine. Best case, I work out a jury rig. Pry the mast out of the step, slide the sail off the mast, and put the sail back on upside-down so the mangled mast foot doesn't have to go back in the step. But first duct-tape the sprit to the crumpled mast as a splint, that can't hurt. Reef the sail by tying together the first three lacing points. Use the sprit boom for a shorter sprit. An oar for a boom.

Ten seconds after landing I'm already tugging the mast out of the step, surprised at how decisive I've become. It's reassuring, this newly discovered capacity for immediate action in the face of a crisis. No dithering now. Bodes well for the rest of the trip.

"Fixing stupid mistakes is one thing," Jagular says. "Not making them in the first place is something else."

"You be quiet," I tell him, still trying to tug the mast out of the step. Boats are passing by as I work things out, asking if I need help. No, I call back. I'm fine. Of course I have no idea if I'm fine or not, but I'm determined to maintain some self-sufficiency, make some attempt to repair the effects of my own stupidity. A few of the Newtons are snickering, rustling around in their packaging. I ignore them. Boats keep passing—fewer now, though, with long stretches where no one passes by at all. We may be last in line.

Just as I'm finishing up a couple of boats pull in to make sure we're ok. There's a friendly guy sailing a lime green proa, and the white-haired sailor who suggested I reef before launching. They offer to help, but I've already managed to get everything mostly rigged. It's ugly, but it should work. The mast is upside-down in the step with the mangled foot at the top where it's out of the way, with the sprit duct-taped to it as a splint; the reefed sail is rolled up into a clumsy bundle at the foot; the boom is in place as a new shorter sprit; and one oar is in place as the new boom.

The proa skipper suggests a better way to tie the mainsheet to the reefed sail, which takes only a few seconds to rig, and then we're ready again. The white-haired sailor with sea-squinty eyes inspects my jury rig without saying anything, leaning in close to check it over.

"I should have tied in a reef like you suggested," I tell him. "I'd have avoided this whole mess. But I guess I kind of need to learn everything the hard way."

"Is there another way?" he says, smiling. We both laugh. I'm about to hop in and set sail when the proa sailor points at my mangled mast.

"You might want to think about rigging a backstay," he suggests politely.

A backstay! That's what I stopped for in the first place, and here I've almost sailed off without it. But it doesn't take long to unstep the mast and use the anchor line to run a backstay from the starboard leeboard cleat to the masthead. Then I re-step the mast and step back to look it over. Afterwards the other sailors launch their boats and sail away with a few final words of encouragement. Apparently they've decided we'll make it. We're alone on the muddy beach again.

"There," I tell Jagular. "That wasn't so bad. What do you think?"

"Well, if there were any doubts about your craftsmanship before," he says, "there are none now."

I shove off the muddy beach and sheet in the new jury-rigged sail, and we're underway again. We slide smoothly down the channel, following the rest of the fleet. Maybe a little slower than before, but we're moving. I eat a couple more of the Newtons, and the rest stop snickering.

♦   ♦   ♦

We reach the camp at Hap's Cut just after sunset and land on the muddy beach alongside the long line of boats already there ahead of us. They're pulled up all along the shore, a misfit armada of homebuilts and aging second-handers, and we've landed at the far end of the line, the latest of the late arrivals. Even the Puddle Ducks came in ahead of us, although at eight feet long they ought to be the slowest boats in the fleet. I realize that the motto on the Texas 200 t-shirts I've seen people wearing—*Lord, let me at least beat the Puddle Ducks*—might not be as much of a joke as I thought.

I walk around a little but nothing seems to be happening except a lot of standing around talking about boats: building boats, fixing boats, building other boats. I'm sick of boats; I've been aboard Jagular for fifteen hours today. Aboard him, or standing beside him in the mud trying to fix him. Finally I wander off to find some supper and a place to sleep. The Duck skippers are standing around in a circle on the beach near my boat, talking loudly. There seems to be rum involved—with them there usually is. I borrow a can opener from one of them. Cold ravioli from a can. Darkness. Unroll sleeping mat on flat sand. Kick off my sandals. Collapse.

TUESDAY

I'm up at dawn for an early launch, easy to do when getting ready means throwing my sleeping bag in Jagular's watertight storage compartment and stepping the duct-taped mast. Then we're off for a relaxing sail down the ICW. With our newly mangled rig, we're a contender for slowest boat of the fleet, but we don't seem to be having any other problems.

"Yet," Jagular says.

"I admire your optimism," I tell the boat.

We're definitely moving slower than we were yesterday. I hook up the self-steering lines and settle in for another long day on the starboard tack. The land slides by, flat and featureless and empty. The wind blows on steadily from the southeast. The sun hangs overhead like a molten hammer, and it's another downwind day as we head north along the treeless shores. Texas.

The new jury-rigged sail is about half the size of the original, so it's downright peaceful to sail with. After a while I get out a notebook and start writing about yesterday's mast fiasco as we sail along. Boat after boat passes us, and I glance up now and then to see that Jagular seems to be following everyone else without any help from me, straight up the ICW's long line of red and green buoys. And then the friendly sailor in the green proa sails by. His boat is moving fast—really fast— and he's busily working the mainsheet and tiller, adjusting the daggerboard, trimming the sails, tightening this and readjusting that. I'm getting tired just watching him. He leans over for a close look at Jagular as he goes past.

"Are you reading a book?" he says, incredulous.

"No," I call back. "Writing one." But he's already gone.

◆   ◆   ◆

The Padre Island Yacht Club, tonight's camp, is a welcome outpost of luxury after Fred Stone Park and Hap's Cut, but the constant jumble of activity makes me feel like I'm in the way. People are scurrying along the docks from one boat to another, and the air-conditioned clubhouse is filled with people fiddling with GPS units and drawing lines on charts, arranging rides into town for tools and supplies, discussing things and repairing things and making plans and back-up plans and alternate plans. After a quick shower and a set of clean clothes, I hang my wet pants on a railing to dry and try to figure out what to do next.

The contrast between the slow silence of sailing and the harried buzz of the Yacht Club is unsettling. All the planning and consulting and chart marking and GPS programming going on here gives me the feeling that there's something I should be doing to prepare for the days ahead, but I don't know what it is. Instead I head back to the boat to grab my shoes. Which aren't there, because I've left them on the beach at Hap's Cut. The dozen or so Raspberry Newtons left in the package chuckle quietly, nudging and elbowing each other.

"Marooned his own shoes, the idjit," I hear one of them say. I eat him, then wonder what to do next.

So far it's been pretty easy, but tomorrow we'll be sailing northward across Corpus Christi Bay and Aransas Bay, our first real stretches of open water, aiming for the remote oyster-shell reef of Paul's Mott. A big day. Big wind, big fetches, maybe some big waves. I pull out my bundle of charts and try to figure out what kind of planning everyone else seems to be doing. It doesn't seem like there's much to do: just keep heading north and don't capsize.

"You ready for tomorrow?" another sailor calls to me as he's walking across the dock, a bundle of gear in his arms, a GPS and handheld radio dangling from one hand, and a laundry bag from the other.

"Sure," I tell him.

WEDNESDAY

I'm up at 5:30. After a quick shower I stow my gear and untie from the dock, then row across the channel and beach Jagular on a nearby island where I'll have room to step the mast and re-rig the backstay. A gray day, and windy. By the time I convince myself I'm ready to face Corpus Christi Bay, there are already some boats ahead of me, heading west down the Yacht Club channel to the ICW. I follow them, risking a couple of short gybes with our jury rig to tack my way downwind.

Today is where the trip gets interesting. It's an easy mile down the ICW to the high bridge where Highway 358 connects Padre Island to the mainland. Maybe a mile after the bridge comes Corpus Christi Bay, a wide stretch of open water, ten miles across. The main channel, the ICW, takes the shortest route, heading almost straight north across the bay. With the winds likely to get stronger as the day goes on, though, anyone going that way could be in for some serious conditions.

Instead, I plan to leave the marked channel as it enters Corpus Christi Bay, cutting east to hug the shore of Mustang Island, the long thin stretch of land separating the ICW from the open waters of the Gulf on this part of our route. On the windward side of the bay near Mustang Island, the waves should be smaller, more suitable for an unballasted boat like Jagular. We'll be threading our way between Mustang Island and Shamrock Island, then on to Stingray Hole, a narrow pass at the northern edge of the bay.

Hugging the shore as I plan to do, it's about nine miles to Stingray Hole. Three hours of sailing, maybe. It will probably be the roughest stretch on the whole trip, and I'm not exactly sure how well the boat will handle it. Jagular is long and lean, only thirty-nine inches wide across the widest part of the flat bottom, and narrow boats don't stand up to wind and waves as well as beamier ones. But Jagular also has decks and large watertight compartments that should protect us from taking on much water, and with our new reefed sail we'll catch a lot less wind than we did on Monday. Finally I decide that the worst that can happen is that I'll be capsized, lose my boat and all my gear, and have a long swim to shore, followed by an even longer walk to someplace where I can buy a bus ticket home. Doesn't sound too bad. If I'm going to be a small boat sailor then I'm going to have to do some sailing. I make sure I have my wallet tucked safely away in the cargo pocket of my shorts and decide I'm ready to give it a try.

By the time we're nearing the high bridge that connects Padre Island to the mainland, I'm caught in the middle of a long procession of boats. Most of them are steadily passing me. There are porpoises popping up everywhere, too, chasing in and out of the other boats, but they avoid us entirely.

"What's with them?" I ask. "Don't they like you?"

"They like me fine," Jagular says. "It's you they're avoiding."

"Why's that?"

"Why does anyone avoid you?" the boat says. "You're always finding fault with the way the world runs. Always complaining about something. And you disagree with everything anyone says."

"No I don't."

"*Quod erat demonstrandum.*"

"All right," I say. "Maybe I do—as if that's such a bad thing. Most of what's wrong with the world is only possible because everyone is afraid to disagree with what's going on around them. But how do all those porpoises know anything about me, anyway?"

"Everyone knows. That's why I'm the only one who'll go sailing with you."

"That's not true," I say.

"Who else?" Jagular demands.

I stop to think about it. "Well. The cat came with us once."

"Yes," Jagular says. "Once."

Our debate dies down as we pass under the bridge and its shadow falls across the cockpit. I'm getting a little nervous. It's only 7:15, but the wind is already strong, stronger than yesterday. My two lasting impressions of the Texas coast: flat and windy.

Soon we'll reach the open waters of Corpus Christi Bay, so I glance around to make sure everything is ship-shape. It's not. When I rigged the backstay this morning, I managed to tie it to the wooden pole duct-taped to the mast. I should have rigged it to the mast itself. Will it hold the way it is? Or will the wind be strong enough to peel the mast away from the improvised splint, crumpling the mast again? I can't make up my mind about what to do, not wanting to waste time stopping but afraid of how little mistakes grow into big ones. Might be better to re-rig it.

Nearing the last of the tiny islands flanking the channel's approach to the open bay, I make my decision: I'll stop to fix the backstay. I steer toward the island, only thirty yards away, and sail right up onto a smooth beach made of millions of crushed oyster shells. Simple enough, and I'm pleased that I've made the smart decision. It's really windy, maybe the windiest day yet—when you're sailing downwind as we are, the wind is always easier to notice when you stop—and it seems to be getting windier. I wouldn't want to lose the mast in the middle of Corpus Christi Bay.

I drag Jagular up out of the water and look around. We're on a perfect marooning island, a low small treeless stretch of sand and weeds lined with oyster shells. Beached here on the southern edge of Corpus Christi Bay, I can look northward across a long stretch of open water, ten miles or more. It's a lonely place. I won't be here long, though. It takes only a few seconds to pull down the mast and adjust the backstay and then I'm ready to go.

It's windy, hard to keep the boat in position for launching, and there's the inevitable shuffling the boat back and forth, trying to hold the bow into the wind as the sail and sprit flap overhead. I adjust the rudder and leeboards, trying not to step into the deep water just offshore. As I'm about to climb aboard, the rudder catches on the bottom just as a gust shoves the bow to port. I hear a distinct crack, a sound like breaking bone, and Jagular gives a small lurch.

Shit—the rudder. That could be an inglorious end to our journey. Plans to rig a steering oar are already flashing through my head as I turn to look, and I wonder if I'll have the nerve to try crossing the bay if I have to steer with the wobbly contraption in my imagination. But it's not the rudder. It's the tiller, broken when it wedged itself against the cockpit side where it couldn't follow the rudder's sudden movement. The rudder is fine.

"That went well," the boat says.

"It could be worse," I tell him.

"It probably will be."

I want to disagree, but he could be right. The rest of the fleet will leave us far behind and it'll be a long slow death by marooning. A couple of the Newtons start chuckling quietly. Ignoring them, I drag Jagular back onto the beach and unstep the mast before inspecting the damages. The tiller is broken cleanly across at the rudder head, almost completely severed. I wiggle it gently and it comes off in my hand, leaving a short stub bolted to the rudder cheeks.

Such a stupid mistake, and so easily avoidable. But already I can see what I have to do: make the new shorter tiller fit between the rudder cheeks, then drill a new bolt hole through the tiller to attach it with. Easy enough. I pull out my Farm & Fleet knife, sit down on the starboard side deck, and start whittling.

As I work, I try not to worry about how I'm going to drill a new hole through the tiller—one thing at a time. I keep whittling. Meanwhile, boat after boat passes my island. Other sailors are shouting to me, asking if I need help. No, I shout back. Not unless you have a quarter-inch drill. No one does. I keep whittling, checking the fit occasionally. Finally I have it; the new tiller, shorter by five inches, fits snugly between the rudder cheeks. Now for the bolt hole.

I fold up my knife and stare at it for a moment. Tucked away alongside the knife blade is the Phillips screwdriver bit. I unfold it. Seems about the right size for a bolt hole. Carefully trying not to expect too much, I jab it into the tiller where the new bolt hole needs to be. It sinks in slightly, and I start to spin it back and forth, using the body of the knife as a handle. After a minute I pull the knife away and examine the result. The start of a hole. This might work.

Twenty minutes later I have a new tiller, shorter but still serviceable. I'm almost getting to like making mistakes just for the simple satisfaction I get from fixing them. Not a very seamanlike attitude but it's all I have.

◆   ◆   ◆

Corpus Christi Bay is bad, the worst conditions we've seen yet. All around us the water is broken into whitecaps, wave after wave after wave, and the wind is still getting stronger. I've cut across the ICW and am heading for the west side of Mustang Island, which means Jagular is almost broadside to the wind and waves now. I'm not sure we're going to make it. Still, for most of the way we'll be less than a mile from Mustang Island, so it's hardly a matter of life and death. Not in water this warm, anyway.

It's a good thing. Already we've seen one boat from the Texas 200 fleet capsize behind us here in Corpus Christi Bay, and another one lose its mast. I'd go back to help but there's no way we can make progress to windward in these conditions—lots of wind, and a sharp chop. And even if I could reach them, Jagular is too small to bring anyone else aboard anyway. They'll have to fend for themselves, or hope help catches up with them.

"That's heroic," says Jagular.

"That's realistic," I tell him. "I'd need a better boat to be a hero. I could swim back to that capsized boat faster than you could get to him. And that other boat probably already called SeaTow on his VHF anyway. No one needs us."

Watching the approaching waves closely to time our turn, I swing us onto our new heading, and we're sailing northward up the shore of Mustang Island. Immediately the boat's motion eases as we start to move downwind rather than across the waves. Before long we're surfing again. Eight miles to go across the bay.

✦   ✦   ✦

We're alone by the time we reach Stingray Hole at the far side of the bay, no other boats in sight ahead or behind. Here there's another choice to make. The simplest route would be to turn right after passing through the hole, following the main shipping channel eastward about a mile, then turning north up the Lydia Ann Channel for another couple of miles. That's the route most of the other boats will be taking.

"But what fun is that?" I ask Jagular. "A paint-by-numbers adventure, sailing from one buoy to the next, following everyone else. We'll head through Corpus Christi Bayou instead."

Corpus Christi Bayou is the back route into Aransas Bay. To get there, we'll pass through Stingray Hole and keep going straight ahead, aiming northeast; any boat able to fit under an eight-foot-high bridge can follow this route, cutting across the shallow backwaters to avoid the big dogleg detour of the shipping channels. We'll sail up to the bridge, where I'll unstep the mast and wade right under it, pulling the boat with me. Once on the other side I'll re-step the mast and we'll follow a twisting, devious route through the series of mudflats and islands that make up Corpus Christi Bayou. If we don't get lost, we should re-join the ICW a few miles further on.

"In theory," the boat says.

I'm more worried about our ability to sail to windward than I am about getting lost, though. We'll have to make some short tacks up some of the channels on the route we've chosen, and I'm not sure how much strain our improvised rig can take. The backstay should help. But with our jury-rigged sail, our windward ability won't be as good as usual, either.

"I wouldn't worry too much about that," Jagular says. "Our windward ability is never that good."

◆   ◆   ◆

We sail through Stingray Hole, cross the shipping lane, and keep heading northeast toward Corpus Christi Bayou. For the first time in the trip I'll be following the chart closely, making sure I know exactly where we are. A chart and a hand compass—the only tools I need. Simplicity, after all, is the foundation of adventure.

"Nonsense," one of the remaining Newtons says. "You're just not smart enough to learn how to use a GPS."

"I *enjoy* navigating with a chart and compass," I say. "If I wanted to push buttons and play video games, I'd stay home on the couch where it's dry and comfortable. Besides, how come you're speaking up now? Where were you out in the bay when it was rough?"

No answer. In retaliation I open the package and eat two of them. They're getting a little soggy.

"What do you expect, taking a boat like this out on Corpus Christi Bay, genius?" one of them says. "Everything is a little soggy."

◆   ◆   ◆

The bridge we're heading for is easy to see, so there's not much navigation involved at first. But it's getting even windier. As we near the bridge I see a crumbling marina at its foot. No boats, just some old wooden docks and a parking lot. I'm not sure if it's still operational, but it makes a convenient place to land. I sail Jagular up onto a boat ramp and hop out, take a look around.

"Look at this," I tell Jagular. "We've come ashore in the middle of an industrial wasteland. A beautiful stretch of barrier islands, remote bays, and deserted beaches, and they've turned it all into a giant refinery. Consume! Consume! Increase production! Grow the economy! And everyone just goes along with it."

"Doesn't the furnace in your basement run on natural gas?" Jagular says.

"When it runs at all. But that doesn't diminish the ugliness of this scene."

An occasional car crosses by on the bridge overhead, and drilling platforms, power lines, refineries and huge factory chimneys line the horizon. All greedily sucking oil and gas from the seabed as quickly as possible and spewing clouds of toxic smoke into the sky.

"The love of oil is the root of all evil," I tell the boat.

"How far did we drive to get to Texas?" he asks. "Twelve hundred miles?"

*   *   *

I unstep the mast and wade under the bridge with Jagular in tow, carefully sidestepping the rocks, broken concrete slabs and mangled rebar that lie under the water. More ugliness, and no less ugly for being hidden under the surface. Again, now that I'm no longer sailing directly downwind, I can feel how windy it is. Once under the bridge I pull the boat up onto the shore and pause to check the chart, and it almost flies away from me as I unfold it. If anything, it's windier now than it was out on Corpus Christi Bay.

From here we have to follow a curving channel that may or may not be marked. If we stray, we'll sail into water so shallow even Jagular won't be able to float. I'm not eager to drag the boat a mile or more through thigh-deep mud if we miss the channel.

Luckily, though, the route begins with a passage between two islands just off the beach—I can see them from where I'm standing. The rest of the channel is marked, on my chart at least, by small white circles that may be pilings or stakes. If they actually exist, the channel should be easy to follow. Time to give it a try. I re-step the mast. The sail flogs crazily; the wind is really ripping. But everything goes smoothly with the launch this time, and soon we're heading down the channel between the two islands.

For a while afterwards the channel is marked, lined with wooden posts that rise about eight feet above the water. Occasionally there are drilling platforms that I can find on the chart, too. Pretty simple stuff. But soon there is nothing, just a broad empty stretch of water that all looks the same. There are scattered islands marked on the chart, but everything is so flat that they're almost impossible to see; they could be islands, or just tall reeds sticking up above the surface of the water.

The sense of space above is enormous, crowding out the land with an emptiness broken only by a few gulls. It's as if the world, flattened by the weight of so much sky, has sunk out of sight beneath us, leaving only the barest tips of things exposed to mark the trail we're trying to follow. I sail by compass headings from the chart, estimating the distance between turns by sheer guesswork. It seems to work, though the rudder bumps the bottom a couple of times and I'm never exactly certain where we are. After a while we come out through a channel between two obvious islands, and we're through the worst of it.

"Compass and chart," I say.

"You got lucky," one of the Newtons says. I eat him.

◆   ◆   ◆

Aransas Bay is rough, too, but once we reach the lee of Mud Island it's not too bad. Should only be about eight or nine miles to the camp at Paul's Mott from here, and for the first time all day the sun breaks free of the clouds. Nothing is quite as scary in bright sunlight. Or maybe the wind is dropping. Maybe both.

By late afternoon I see a clump of masts on the horizon. Soon afterward I see the camp, a long finger of oyster-shell reef sticking out into Aransas Bay from the barrier island to our east. There are boats pulled up all along the reef and anchored offshore. I steer around the point and approach from the downwind side where we'll have some shelter from the waves. Several people wade out to meet us. Together we lift Jagular all the way out of the water, setting him on the end of the reef, between the Hobie catamaran and the green proa. Jagular's stern hangs cantilevered out over the waves, a foot above sea level. We're high and dry on Paul's Mott. We've made it.

"This far, anyway," Jagular says.

THURSDAY

I'm up early, waiting for my turn at the clump of bushes a ways down the beach that's serving as the head for a bunch of us this morning. Between dodging the rattlesnakes and finding a convenient bush it makes for a later launch than usual, and many boats are already heading out by the time I manage to organize my gear and slide Jagular into the water. Got to wear long pants today—yesterday afternoon's sun gave me a good start at a burn. I start rummaging through my gear for my one pair of long pants. Which aren't there, because they're still draped over the railing at the Padre Island Yacht Club where I left them.

This time I eat a couple of the Newtons before they even have time to start snickering—call that breakfast. Then I decide the missing pants don't matter too much anyway; I'll just wrap my sleeping mat over my legs for some instant shade. But I'm wondering how much of my gear will end up strewn all along the Texas coast by the end of the week.

I'm too tired to really care, though. Before it was even fully dark last night I collapsed on the oyster-shell reef beside Jagular and fell asleep. No need to stay up all night making repairs like some of the other sailors have been doing; I've had all my problems already. At least I hope so. But by now I have some confidence in my ability to muddle through despite making mistakes, anyway. I'm starting to feel like I belong here.

I've made another discovery, too: I really enjoy spending the long hours sailing alone. I suppose some might find it boring to spend all day alone, moving so slowly, but I seem to be immune to boredom aboard a small boat of my own. These long slow passages—thirty or forty miles a day, the longest I've ever sailed in a small boat by far—seem to offer an antidote to the mad rushing that marks so much of our lives. Alone for so long in a small boat like Jagular, my mind's clumsy and unceasing clamoring is slowly worn down until nothing remains but a simple awareness of the moment—a moment that stretches on for eight, nine, ten hours of solitude. No need for thinking, only being. The sound of the waves. The feel of the tiller. The motion of the boat through the water. And always, the wind. Sailing alone is life reduced to a perfectly elegant simplicity.

After launching, we follow a line of boats northwest toward the day's first challenge: a series of three passes that will take us through the shallows of Carlos Bay and Mesquite Bay. I'm looking forward to finally leaving the well-marked ICW behind and doing some real navigating. I manage to pass a few boats by cutting close in across the shallows at the west end of Jaybird Reef, and then we're at the entrance to the first pass, just off Dunham Island. For once in this flat flat land it's easy to recognize features from the chart—Cape Carlos, then Cedar Point—and I'm a little disappointed to have a line of boats in front of me to follow. Takes some of the satisfaction out of finding my way through. Again, though, I'm given a little boost of confidence in my chart-and-compass navigating. No need for anything else.

"You're an idiot," one of the Newtons says. "Magellan, Shackleton, Cook—they used the best navigation technology they could get. They would have loved a GPS."

I ignore him; it's too nice a day to fight back. It's not long before we're through Cedar Dugout, the second pass, and then I'm following a long line of boats strung out across Mesquite Bay, heading generally eastward toward the narrow cut of Ayres Dugout. With our jury rig we can barely hold this course—we can't manage much more than a beam reach. I start trying to angle us to windward a little, putting something in the bank in case we miss the cut, but I can see it's going to be close.

Then up ahead, between me and the island that must mark the entrance to Ayres Dugout, I see waves breaking in shallow water, always an unsettling sight. And on the far side of the shoals, the island we're aimed at turns out to be two or three separate islands separated by marshy channels. There are a number of boats pulled up on the beach of the westernmost island, but I'll have to get past the reef to get there. I tuck my chart away without really looking at it, trying to make out what's happening up ahead. Again I try unsuccessfully to head more to windward, guessing that the beached boats have missed the channel at Ayres Dugout by being caught too far downwind. They must've landed on the island to regroup. Why else would they stop?

I aim for the passage between the islands, but I can already tell we're not going to make it. The wind is driving Jagular toward the shallow reefs ahead, and we can't point high enough to sail around them. Soon the rudder is bumping the bottom, then the leeboards. Then we're stopped, aground on a mound of oyster shells in ankle deep water two hundred and fifty yards off the beach.

As Jagular grinds to a halt, the full force of the wind hits me again. Windy! Now that I'm stopped I can really feel it, blowing hard. I pull on some flip-flops I borrowed from another sailor and quickly hop out of the boat to pull down the sprit and furl the sail, then unstep the mast and stow it aboard. The water is so shallow that even without me aboard Jagular won't float free. The wind is pushing the boat onto the leeboard and rudder, driving them hard into the oyster-shell bottom. I pull off the rudder, then untie both leeboards and stow everything aboard before starting to tug Jagular toward the island. The hull scrapes across the surface of the reef, but pulls easily enough. Probably weighs less than two hundred pounds, even fully loaded as it is.

I haven't taken more than a few steps before the oyster shells have cut my feet up pretty badly, though—the muddy bottom keeps sucking the flip-flops off my feet, and the shells are sharp-edged and cruel. Feels like walking through a huge tub of knee-deep butter filled with thousands of pieces of broken glass. Still, the flip-flops are far better than nothing. I manage to make my way across the reef, stopping every few steps to pull the flip-flops back unto my feet, and in a few minutes I reach a narrow deep-water channel that separates the reefs from the island. I don't bother to get back in the boat, crowded with oars, rudder, leeboards, and rig; I just start swimming, pulling Jagular behind me like a dog on a leash. It only takes a few minutes to reach the shore, where I pull the boat up beside a Hobie catamaran and check my feet.

Not too bad after all—I'm bleeding from a number of cuts and scrapes, but only one bad wound, a three-inch laceration sliced deep into the meat of my right heel. I rinse it with fresh water and carefully press the flap of skin back over the cut and duct tape it shut. Seems to work. Then I head up the narrow beach to where a number of people have gathered at a cabin on the island.

It's a surreal transition, not at all what I expected to find here in the middle of nowhere. Someone is cooking breakfast in the cabin, offering food to all takers. Others are talking on handheld VHF radios, trying to warn people about the reefs. Still others are watching the approaching boats, a long line of them strung out from Cedar Dugout to the island. I wander around aimlessly for a while, not really sure why so many of us have gathered here. Lots of the boats behind me seem to be having problems. A Puddle Duck runs aground way out on the reef, and a couple of people wade out to help. Meanwhile the radio chatter grows more animated as everyone tries to figure out what's happening. "Go more to windward than you are," someone says. Another radio voice disagrees. Someone else comes on to ask what's going on. Utter confusion.

Finally I decide I might as well get moving. "Where's the cut?" I ask the Hobie cat sailor. "Between the islands, right? I think I'll just drag my boat back there along the beach, shouldn't be too hard."

He stares at me for a second. "Dude," he says, pointing at the deep channel running past the island just a few feet offshore—the channel I swam across a few minutes before. "The cut's right there. That's it."

What the… I go back to my boat and pull out my compass. The channel I swam across runs almost due north; I'm sure that on my chart, Ayres Dugout runs east to west. The Hobie guy can't be right. He is, though. I understand as soon as I pull out my chart to check. I've been fooled, not noticing how the island angles northeast instead of straight north. There is no passage between the islands, no need to fight to windward. I just have to sail around the west side of the whole group, right down the deep channel alongside the beach.

If I could have gained just a little more ground to windward, I would've sailed right around the eastern edge of the reefs, where a turn to the left would have put me safely in the channel without running aground. Either way, though,

I've made it now. Home free. But I'm annoyed with myself for following the boats ahead of me instead of my chart. It wouldn't have made much difference here—with Jagular unable to work to windward, I would have ended up aground on the reef anyway—but I decide it's the last time I'll let something like that happen. No more mindless following! I re-rig the rudder and leeboards, step the mast, and I'm off down the channel.

◆   ◆   ◆

After sailing past a few small islands, we round the corner into San Antonio Bay. There's a sailboat way up ahead, its sails barely visible over the horizon. I set my self-steering gear and follow it directly across the bay, aiming for Panther Point. This course takes us away from the lee of Matagorda Island, into open water, but we seem to be doing fine. Along the way we pass several gas drilling platforms, intricate masses of pipes and tubes that rise from the shallow bay like sets of abandoned monkey bars. They're much smaller than I imagined.

"More vampiracy," I tell the boat. "The love of oil really is the root of all evil, see? We're slowly and steadily sucking the life from everything we touch, even here in the middle of a remote bay, far from any roads or cities."

"Don't even start," Jagular says.

"If you want to bury your head in the sand, go ahead." But I'm too lazy to say more, too contented. It's a beautiful day. Soon the drilling platforms drop out of sight behind us.

Six miles later we reach Panther Point, where an exposed oyster shell reef reaches from deep out in the bay toward shore like a bony and beckoning finger. There are hundreds of hunched-over birds lined up in the shallows all along the way, a curmudgeonly bunch, surly and grumbling. Luckily there's a narrow channel of deeper water just off the point, so we're able to sail right past them between Panther Point and the reef just a few yards offshore.

About a mile and a half past Panther Point, I angle further offshore, following a compass course toward South Pass. At least, toward the place that South Pass is supposed to be, according to my chart—as always around here, the islands are too low to see. About four miles straight ahead if I'm doing this right.

"You're not," one of the Newtons says. "Smart sailors use a GPS."

Another Newton chimes in. "And your insistence on clinging to outdated technologies isn't evidence of any moral superiority on your part, you know. It's only a symptom of your psychotic compulsion toward non-conformity."

"Hey, what's with the constant negativity?" I ask. "Because look at this wind, these waves, this sun! When are you going to stop complaining?"

"When are you going to stop eating us?" the first Newton says.

"Circle of life," I tell him. "We're all part of someone's food chain."

"There are only eight of us left, you know."

"Don't be such a baby," I say. But I put the carton away without eating any of them. They're getting too soggy anyway.

◆   ◆   ◆

Once we're through South Pass and into Espiritu Santo Bay we run into problems again. The wind has shifted to the northeast, directly offshore. And it's picking up. By the time I make out the distant group of buildings that must be Army Hole, the abandoned Army Air Corps base that's tonight's destination, I'm wondering if we'll make it. We're sailing a beam reach parallel to the shore, but we can't point high enough to get any closer. The waves are building, making it even harder to make any progress to windward. The chop is getting big enough to be exciting. If I don't figure something out soon we're going to end up in the marshes two miles past Army Hole.

I mess around trying everything I can think of for an hour or so, but with this mangled jury rig it's just not going to work. The wind is much stronger now, the waves tossing Jagular sharply, sending plenty of spray aboard. And it's getting late, not much daylight left. Finally I give up. We'll have to sail the best course we can manage until we hit the buoyed channel leading into Army Hole and figure out what to do from there. I can always row in, or tie up to a buoy for the night. Or keep going and camp in the marshes down the coast. Something. So it's back to a beam reach on the starboard tack for now.

Once we give up our feeble attempts to fight the wind, we move along smartly, paralleling the shoreline. It's not long before we hit the channel at marker 21, about a mile offshore and directly in line with the entrance to the Army Hole harbor. Moving quickly, I pull down the rig and stow it for rowing.

"You weren't that quick, actually," Jagular says.

He's right. I should have tied off to the buoy first and then dropped the sail. By the time I start to row, the wind has pushed us a hundred yards further offshore. No matter. We'll get there eventually. I start rowing toward shore, dead upwind.

It only takes a few strokes before I know how much of an ordeal this is going to be, though. I can hardly move the boat at all, and on each recovery it's almost as hard to pry the oars through the air as it is to pull the boat through the water.

"It'd be nice if you could feather the oars," Jagular says. "Too bad you used those cheap pinned oarlocks from the hardware store."

I'm working too hard to answer. Each oar blade becomes a sail as soon as I lift it from the water, pushing us backwards. And it's not easy timing the strokes in this chop; a couple of times my oars bite nothing but air, throwing me off balance. We're making no progress at all. At least no one's coming out to offer us a tow. I'd probably refuse, and then feel stupid about it after it was too late. But I suppose it's dark enough by now that no one could see us even if they were looking this way.

"We're not going to make it," Jagular says after a while.

An unreasonable stubbornness grabs me, defeating my natural inclinations toward laziness.

"We'll make it," I say. "I'm sleeping ashore at Army Hole tonight, even if I have to swim there."

The conventional wisdom on rowing into a stiff wind, I remember reading somewhere, is to shorten your stroke, like downshifting a bike to ride up a steep hill. I try it for one hundred strokes, take a ten-second rest, then give it another hundred. No good—we're not losing ground, but we're not getting anywhere either. Still about a mile to go.

I try the opposite instead, taking as long and slow a stroke as I can manage. It's slow and exhausting and probably poor technique, but we're moving. Barely. I continue for fifty strokes, then pause. Definite progress.

"Hell with it then," I say aloud, and start rowing in earnest, long slow strokes that push the boat slowly through the wind and water. Every so often a particularly large wave sends a shower of spray over the bow onto my back. I count a hundred strokes, rest for a few seconds, then a hundred more. Another hundred. Turn around to look—we're closer now, but my look back just cost us a few yards. I give it another hundred. Getting darker. Blisters forming. Another hundred strokes. And another hundred. I turn to look. Half a mile to go. Plus the distance I just lost by looking. I start another hundred strokes. Somewhere in the cockpit the surviving Newtons start jeering, but I'm too busy to retaliate.

◆   ◆   ◆

I row into Army Hole's inner harbor in the darkness, completely exhausted and almost asleep at the oars. Several people help me tie up to a dock that's way too high for Jagular. Tired as I am, I can barely climb up onto the pier, dragging a random pile of food and gear with me. Someone from another boat asks me if there's anything he can do to help. I'm grateful, but so tired all I can do is mumble an unintelligible reply and stagger off barefoot through the sandburs that lie scattered around the lawn like land mines. I barely feel them.

I drop my sleeping mat on the ground in the middle of the lawn and collapse on top of it for a while before I can find the energy to grab something from my food bag. Sardines in mustard sauce, the first thing I pull out. I pry open the can and start eating. I'm asleep almost before I finish them.

FRIDAY

I lie on the ground staring blankly at nothing for a few minutes before I realize I'm awake. It's as good as over. Today should be an easy day, only twenty miles or so. I slowly pull myself out from under my thin blanket and stand up, stretching my back and arms. I've slept in today, tired from last night's rowing. It looks like everyone else is already up. Moving slowly, I limp across the grass to hang yesterday's damp shirt on a fence overlooking the harbor, give it a chance to dry before I leave.

In honor of our last day I pull on my Ironman Wisconsin t-shirt, which has the word FINISHER written in large bold letters across the back. Seems appropriate again today—I feel like I've just finished something, that's for sure. Then, reluctant to let the journey end, I take a long walk around Army Hole. No reason to hurry now.

But Army Hole is flat and windy, and overrun with huge jackrabbits who hop around eyeing everyone with murderous intent. Before long I'm ready to get started, so I stow my gear aboard Jagular and cast off, rowing out to the harbor entrance. A fellow sailor holds the bow line while I step the mast and set the spritsail, then tosses me the line when I'm ready. The offshore wind blows us off the dock and I sheet in on the port tack—port tack at last, after four days!—as we glide into the open water of Espiritu Santo Bay for the last passage.

From Army Hole the buoyed channel takes a V-shaped track, angling left and then back right to rejoin the main ICW. But we'll ignore the channel, sail straight past the tip of Grass Island instead, on the edge of the maze of drilling platforms clustered inside the V. The winds are light, the water calm, a perfect day. I take a compass heading from the chart, aiming for channel marker 13. It's out of sight way up ahead, a final exam in pilotage. I set the self-steering lines and lie back in the cockpit, dozing. Still tired. Every once in a while I look around. An occasional drilling platform to port. Grass Island to starboard. Most of the other boats have stuck to the channel and are well left of our course.

I sail across the bay for about an hour without ever touching the tiller before I see the buoy dead ahead. Still not touching the tiller, I watch it get closer and closer. A green channel marker. Still dead ahead, right on our compass heading. I watch, fascinated, as Jagular's self-steering lines tug the tiller back and forth, zeroing in on the buoy. Much closer now, I can almost read the number.

Unbelievable—it's a 13.

We sail directly toward the buoy, a collision course. As we come within a boat length of the buoy I unhook the self-steering lines and push the tiller to port. Jagular angles away, passing so close to the buoy that I can reach out and touch it. The last few Newtons remain conspicuously silent.

◆   ◆   ◆

Later that evening, ashore at Magnolia Beach, I watch the Puddle Ducks arrive. They never made it to Army Hole. They waited too long at Ayres Dugout, pulling boats off the reef, acting like heroes—a role that seems to fit them surprisingly well considering their crude little sandbox-boats and endearingly misfit status—and ended up camping on a god-awful spoil island somewhere, alone in the vast emptiness of the Texas coast while the rest of the fleet rested at Army Hole. Now they're sailing onto the beach like Lindbergh landing in Paris. Jagular and I left Ayres Dugout just in time to miss it all.

"See that welcome?" I say. "That could be us. We should have stayed behind and helped pull all those sinking ships off the reef."

"Don't go trying to make us into heroes," the boat says. "We're lucky we made it at all."

He's probably right. I didn't want to spend the day standing around in those oyster-shell reefs getting my feet all sliced up anyway. The water here is probably filled with flesh-eating bacteria and petroleum-based chemical waste. My heroism, such as it is, has limits.

"That's for sure," Jagular says. "Like those capsized and dismasted boats in Corpus Christi Bay that you wouldn't turn back for."

"We wouldn't have made it," I tell him. "You're not a good enough boat."

"It's not the boat, it's the captain," he says.

Maybe so. But we did make it, after all. Port Mansfield to Magnolia Beach. Five days and almost two hundred miles and we're still afloat despite everything that went wrong. We may have done some dumb things but we didn't give up. Maybe that's enough.

And now the Puddle Ducks are here, too, the last of the fleet, the rag-tag rum-swilling rearguard of the Texas 200, and every one of us is down at the water's edge watching them come in and probably wishing we were with them. One by one they sail up onto the beach where people are cheering and applauding and taking pictures and stepping forward to lift the little boats ashore. The last Duck skipper steps onto the sand to drag his boat up onto dry land and the crowd cheers a last cheer and the sun drops below the horizon and people take a few last photographs and then it's over.

I wander up and down the beach all the rest of the evening trying to hold something of the past few days in my mind, listening to stories from my fellow sailors, watching them pack up their boats and gear. Jagular is already back on the trailer for the long drive back to Wisconsin. The wind is dying down. The sky is slowly filling with the first faint stars of evening.

We made it. Nothing heroic or particularly impressive about that, but still, it's immensely satisfying. To have come so far—forty or fifty miles each day, serious distance for a boat like Jagular—and to have been so much at home in the doing of the thing, living the way sailors have always lived, in long slow hours filled with an abundance of time and solitude that life ashore rarely measures out with such generosity. We've done all right, Jagular and I, to have travelled so far together, farther than any map or chart can measure. Farther than I expected.

As it gets darker I walk over to where a few people have started a fire on the beach. The flames glow brightly in the shadows, casting flickering shadows across the sand, creating a small circle of light in the immense darkness that surrounds us all. It's a nice place to end up, even if the Puddle Duckers are breaking into the rum again. I suppose they've earned it, sailing those ridiculous little boats all this way. I'm just starting to think about laying my sleeping mat beside the fire so I can drift off to sleep when another sailor approaches from somewhere down the beach. It's dark now, and he leans in close to be sure it's me.

"This is yours, isn't it?" he says. "I think I saw you wearing it before." He holds up the shirt I left hanging on the fence at Army Hole this morning. Far across the beach, buried in the back of my car, the last few Newtons start laughing.

Jagular at Swan Lake

"Let's go," I tell the boat, sliding it off the grassy bank and into the water.

"Are you crazy? It's 4:30 a.m."

"Best part of the day," I say, climbing down into the cockpit and setting the oars in their sockets. The left oarlock is squeaking again so I pull it out and spit on the pin to lube it. Should work for a while.

Here on the upper Fox River the silence is broken only by small marshy sounds: chirping frogs, singing birds, the gurgling of the water sliding past in the near darkness—a squeaking oarlock would be blasphemy. Long fingers of mist slide through the reeds and along the surface of the water, revealing little, promising everything. The world is ours, the river our road to whatever small adventure we can find before breakfast.

Back in the campground dozens of double-axle campers sit side by side in their campsites like fat hogs crammed into pens, each stuffed with all the oppressive conveniences of home. Bug zappers, rattling generators, bright lights. King-size beds, full kitchens, bathrooms, air conditioning, DVD players, big-screen TVs and video games. Camping has become a war of relentless one-upmanship, and last night the assaults never ended. Buy more stuff! buzzed the night lights. You need it! rattled the generators. Consume and be happy! called the patio furniture beside each camper. An

easier life is a better life! insisted the automatic coffee mak-
ers and the microwave ovens. Comfort is king! sang the
reclining camp chairs around each fire ring.

"The hell with you," I told them. "I'm leaving."

✦   ✦   ✦

"You can't even see where we're going," the boat points out as
I'm bundling the sail, mast, and sprit into the cockpit in case
we make it all the way downstream to Swan Lake. We should
be able to do some sailing there if we find any wind.

"The sun will be up sooner than you think," I say. "And
besides, there's plenty of light, you just have to let your eyes
adjust. And remember to look at things out of the corner of
your eye, that's where all the cones are. Or the rods. Whatever. Just don't look directly at things." I start rowing down
the narrow creek. A few moments later the boat scrapes across
a sandbar and grinds to a gentle stop.

"Is that why we ran aground just then?" the boat asks.
"Because you weren't looking out of the corner of your eye?"

"When did you get to be such a smartass?" I ask, poking at the sandy bottom with an oar. After an initial show
of resistance Jagular pivots back into the current and slides
slowly downstream into an overhanging tree. The branches
scratch at my face and shoulders, doing their best to throw
me overboard. I duck into the cockpit and the boat scrapes
awkwardly past.

"Who even told you this section of the river was naviga-
ble?" asks the boat once we are floating freely again.

"Who told me? Who told me? Why does everyone have to
be told everything these days?" I say. "Whatever happened to
finding things out for yourself?"

"It's just that the water seems to be only ankle-deep."

"We're floating, aren't we?"

"And the river is so narrow you can barely fit both oars

into the water," the boat continues, ignoring me. "The channel's pretty twisty, too, and filled with sunken logs and fallen branches." I ignore him back, pulling smoothly at the oars. We move silently downstream into the darkness and the sounds of the marsh.

◆   ◆   ◆

A hint of light colors the sky now, and the winding channel of the river cuts like a shining ribbon through hummocks of tall grass and scattered stands of oak and hickory. Too swampy to build on and too muddy and inconvenient to walk through, the marsh is a sanctuary. No lights. No trucks. No generators. No people.

There are few signs of human influence here at all, no right angles or straight lines; the shortest distance between two points has become irrelevant. The grass bends in gentle curves. The trees lean comfortably this way and that, and the river itself has more twists than a corkscrew. Each hairpin carves a deep channel along the outside edge where the current runs swiftest; the inside edges form long sandbars jutting out into the river. North for twenty yards, then a sharp bend. Southeast for thirty yards, another sharp bend. North for fifteen yards. South for twenty. And so it goes. The river is in no hurry to reach a destination. Better to wander freely here rather than to rush on to the series of dams and locks that control the Fox further north, where the river has been tamed.

Actually, this section of the Fox River is an anomaly, a winding marshy stream that obscures the river's history as a major transportation corridor. Just ten miles down the river, past Swan Lake, is the town of Portage. That's where the first white men in Wisconsin—Jesuit explorers traveling upstream from Lake Michigan—dragged their boats overland from the Fox to the nearby Wisconsin River and on to the Mississippi, bringing God, smallpox, and French place names to the New World. I try to imagine what it must have been like here in the seventeenth century, when rivers ran through forests so extensive that a squirrel could travel from northern Wisconsin to the coast of Maine without ever touching the ground.

"We've ruined that, too," I tell the boat. "Fly an airplane over this country and you'll see. We've carved the entire continent into squares and rectangles: roads, housing developments, cities, towns, fields, malls, parking lots, factories, airports, highways. Whatever small pieces of the natural world that remain are wedged in between the golf courses and strip malls. The only escape is to stick to tiny swampy rivers like this one and pretend that the thread of unspoiled land along the banks is more than a pleasant illusion. If any other species dug their homes and burrows and trails all over the landscape the way we do, we'd call it a plague, an infestation! But when we do it, we call it Progress."

"Why do you have to be so surly?" the boat asks.

"In a world where plagues are progress, surliness is sanity," I say, and go back to scanning the marsh around me. I know it's only a pretend wilderness, a bit of undeveloped land squeezed into a crooked corner of the map, but the illusion is a good one. Two cranes, startled by our approach, lurch clumsily into the sky and fly away. Around another corner a whitetail deer stares at us as I row past. A barred owl calls, and I hoot back until I round the next bend and see him fly away.

The river is barely wide enough to allow both oars in the water, but the current helps. At each bend it pushes the stern around while I row with the outside oar to keep Jagular's nose pointed down the channel. Then we're through and I can take half a dozen strokes with both oars before the next bend sweeps us around in the opposite direction.

Already this trip is reminding me how much I love rowing. It's a perfect integration of man and machine, supreme efficiency on an unabashedly human scale. Meditation through motion. I pull, and the boat glides smoothly across the water. Press down on the handles to lift the oar blades a few inches, then push forward. The oars swing backward in a smooth arc, scattering droplets of water that splash a curving path of expanding rings across the surface of the river. I lean forward and let the weight of the oars push my hands ever so slightly upward until the blades settle gently into the water. Repeat. Repeat. Repeat. There are intricate subtleties of grip and nuanced motion to play with, but the principle is brilliant in its simplicity. Smooth silent motion propelled by human muscle and leverage alone.

"Progress is a myth," I tell the boat. "Every new technology introduced since the invention of rowing has been a step backward."

"That's blatant hypocrisy coming from someone sitting in a plywood boat glued together with high-tech two-part epoxy adhesives, rigged with a sail made from polyethylene tarp, and transported on a trailer pulled by a gasoline-powered automobile," Jagular says.

"It's not quite as hypocritical as you think," I say. "I didn't use epoxy—you're a temporary boat, remember? Besides, hypocritical or not, it's true. Our lives are too easy for our own good. We flip a switch, twist a throttle, press down on a foot pedal and unleash the forces of infernal combustion for our convenience. Meanwhile we get fatter and weaker and less imaginative, less able to do anything for ourselves."

"Are you finished yet?" the boat asks.

"Yes, I am." I pull hard on the starboard oar and spin the boat around to a neat stop alongside a sandbar, plunge an oar into the sand, and clove-hitch the painter to it.

"You know, a real painter hooks onto a bow eye," the boat

says. "What you have there is just a ratty piece of quarter-inch line tied off to the cleat for the lateen rig you don't use any more."

"Are you finished yet?"

"Almost," Jagular says. "Now where was I? Oh, yes—the lateen rig you don't use any more because you kept capsizing us with it." The boat stops to think for a moment. "Now I'm done."

"Thank you." I step off onto the sandbar and immediately sink to my knees in thick mud. "Hey! I thought you said the bottom was sandy."

"There might be some mud," the boat admits.

◆   ◆   ◆

The day grows lighter, but the channel is getting more difficult to navigate. Fallen logs. Broad sandbars blocking all but a narrow stream of deeper water along the edge. A tiny ripple of rapids where the river squeezes between two fallen trees. Impossible, I think, and then find a way through. I feel a perverse satisfaction at getting Jagular past each unlikely stretch without climbing out of the boat and wading.

At one point I stand up, pull an oar out and use it to pole our way between two logs jammed tightly together in the center of the channel, and then shove hard to build up enough momentum to get us halfway over the next log. From there I'm able to shift my weight back and forth until the boat works its way over the log and is floating again. "Just think of it," I tell the boat. "We must be the first ones ever to row this stretch of the river."

"That isn't necessarily something to brag about," Jagular says.

We continue downstream. Sunrise arrives unnoticed, lost in gray clouds. The channel is wider now, and straighter. Up ahead a lone fencepost stands on the bank like a sentinel, a few strands of barbed wire clinging to the weathered wood. Just past the post a low railroad bridge crosses the river. I tether Jagular to an oar shoved into the mud and get out to have a look.

The bridge is in ruins. Only a few massive steel beams remain, resting on crumbling concrete piers. The ties and rails have been removed, and the skeletal bridge reaches only halfway across the river. I climb onto the rusting I-beams and walk out to the end to stare down at my reflection in the water below. A bridge to nowhere—except for the rickety foot bridge laid across the missing span, allowing access to the east bank.

"I suppose this is where you start bemoaning the spread of industrial civilization again," the boat calls. "Railroads and bridges and I-beams, oh my."

"On the contrary," I say. "I was just thinking that this dead-end bridge is a perfect metaphor for the inevitable decline of our dead-end civilization." I look out at the marsh, listening to the birds and frogs, the water flowing by, the wind slipping through the tall grass. "The Age of Oil is coming to an end. The rattle and clank of machinery, the rumble of engines, the choking fumes will fade. The natural world will take over. Our lives will improve as civilization returns to a more human scale."

"You're crazy."

"Nope. It's already happening. Someone built this foot bridge, didn't they? With no fuss and no machines, someone carried in these two-by-fours, a hammer and some nails, and built a bridge to a new world, one founded on a sensibly human scale, free from the greedy demands and complications of industrial technology. A new civilization built on the remnants of the old."

I turn to look at the boat floating lazily by the riverbank. "A world where wooden boats will have to earn their keep."

"What keep? You haven't painted me or varnished my decks since you built me."

"I didn't varnish you then, either," I say, "and you're still afloat, aren't you?" No answer. I turn to look more closely at the rusting bridge. Moss is already sprouting from the concrete, the heavy anchor bolts are crooked and corroding, the steel is rusting. In the gap between the I-beams, a spider web catches the sun, delicate threads glistening with dew. A sparrow flutters under the bridge and stops at a midstream rock for a drink.

"See?" I say. "The world will heal itself, given enough time, without regard for human civilization. The damage that we're doing will be erased in the long run."

"Uh-huh," Jagular says. "A spider web and a bird on a rock. Nature triumphs."

"I can't help it," I tell him. "I honestly believe that our civilization is doomed. I'm an optimist."

"Murphy was an optimist, too. Look where it got him."

◆   ◆   ◆

Not far past the bridge the river widens; Swan Lake must be just ahead. I row across the glassy water whistling the theme from Tchaikovsky's famous ballet.

"What are you doing?" Jagular says. "Don't you know it's bad luck to whistle aboard a sailing ship?"

"First of all, you're not a ship, you're a boat." I stop rowing. "And second, that's the theme from Tchaikovsky's *Swan Lake*. I thought it was fitting, considering that we've arrived." And we have. The lake opens up around us, its surface smooth and polished as black ice.

"And look," I point out. "Swans." There are two of them, gliding across the water with a regal dignity. Magnificent birds. Beautiful and majestic.

"Maybe you should get your eyes checked," the boat says.

"Those are geese."

"Ok, they're geese," I say. "But they're still beautiful graceful birds. And besides, I'm not going to let you spoil my day. We've made it—we managed to row the Fox River all the way to Swan Lake. While everyone else was still asleep in their campers, we've gone out and discovered an adventure. We've seen cranes, owls, deer, turtles, rowed several miles of the river that have probably never been rowed before, and still have the return journey to look forward to. With luck we'll get back to the campground just as everyone else is finishing the breakfast dishes."

"I thought we were going to go sailing," the boat says.

I look out at the water. Not a ripple, no hint of a breeze. "Sorry. Not this time, I guess."

Jagular chuckles. "That's probably for the best," he says.

"Why's that? I thought you liked sailing."

"I do." Another chuckle. "But it usually helps to have the rudder and leeboards."

I glance around the cockpit—no leeboards, no rudder hanging from the transom. "You mean you let me come all this way to go sailing when you knew I didn't have the stuff along? Why didn't you say anything?"

"Hey, you're the captain. I'm just a boat," Jagular says, and starts whistling the theme from *Swan Lake*. We spin slowly around in the current. The geese disappear around a corner and we're left alone in the middle of the lake, drifting aimlessly.

Back in the campground the early risers are beginning to think about getting up. The night lights are winking out, the bug zappers are falling silent. Somewhere a venetian blind flicks open, and a coffee maker churns to life with a whir and a click. With a sigh I take the oars and start to row back.

Jagular's Wild Ride

"IT'S AWFULLY DA—"

A wave splashes aggressively into the cockpit midsentence, cutting me off as it drenches me again. Everything is wet through, my clothes a sodden mess, my sunglasses knocked half off my face by the spray. We're sailing through a fast-moving frontal system that's tumbling down into Potagannissing Bay from Canada, pushing before it a fierce wind that has Jagular thudding along into the chop with more than his usual lack of finesse. The watertight compartment in the bow booms hollowly as it hits each wave, an echo chamber sounding an increasingly funereal drumbeat. Cold water sloshes ankle-deep across the cockpit floor, adding to the boat's unsettling motion. Four miles to go before we can duck into the relatively sheltered bay east of Fairbank Point.

And we've got a reef tied in, which means this is as good as it's going to get—we're still a bit sheltered here in the lee of Gull Island. We're about to sail out into the open, into the full force of the wind. Suddenly the boat ducks headfirst into a particularly large and obnoxious wave, sending an alarming cascade of what used to be Lake Huron over the foredeck into the cockpit.

There's a long way to go. I figure there's about a fifty-fifty chance we'll make it.

◆　　　◆　　　◆

The morning started out without much of a breeze, just enough to move us along gently. A perfect day for sailing across the tiny inlet of Potagannissing Bay where we'd rented a cottage for the week. I even managed to convince my wife to accompany us in her kayak. We can have a picnic at the town park beach on the bay's eastern shore, I suggested. It'll be fun.

The suggestion of a picnic was a tactical move, an acknowledgement of the inordinate pleasure my wife derives from packing and unpacking things, arranging and repacking and combining and rearranging them in esoteric configurations to take up the least possible space. A picnic basket, to her, is an opportunity to impose order upon the universe. There'd be soft cheeses, I knew. Crisp rice crackers. Fresh fruit. Dried fruit. Tiny cheese knives, and fruit knives, and cloth napkins, and sauces, and spreads. Runcible spoons, for all I know. Crusty baguettes. Exotic condiments. Hummus. Olives stuffed with garlic. Olives stuffed with bleu cheese. Olives stuffed with olives. Olive tapenade. Fancy mustards and chutneys—the more accoutrements the better.

The lack of accoutrements is exactly what I like about sailing.

"Don't worry, we'll wait for you," I promise. "We won't go too far ahead. It's only a couple of miles across the bay anyway, even if we do get separated. You'll be fine."

•   •   •

"I thought you said we were going to wait for her," Jagular says, watching my wife paddle off into the distance ahead of us. Again.

"She's cheating," I say. "Paddling like that. It's shameless."

But eventually a northwesterly breeze fills in little by little, and soon we're catching up again, weaving through the chain of small islands scattered along our path to the far side of the bay. The sun is hot, the water pleasantly cool as I trail my fingertips along the surface. I have the sheet cleated and the tiller tied off and Jagular is steering himself. The new balance lug rig seems to be working well. Without any effort from me, our motion scribes a shining line across the clear green water.

So nice to be enveloped in silence again. No, not silence; just the small sounds of sailing. The boat slipping through the water. The leeboards creaking. The wind. We're on a broad reach now, Jagular's best point of sail, so I ease the sheet to catch more of the breeze, feeling again the joyful synergy of the air's pull, a motion fueled entirely by sunlight and the earth's rotation. Air heats up, and rises. More air pours in from elsewhere to fill the empty space, is deflected by the earth's spin, collides with other currents, is channeled by topography into whorls and eddies and countercurrents. Sun. Wind. Gravity. Water. There's an exquisite serenity in harnessing so much wild energy at so little cost, and at such high efficiency. We've left my wife and her plastic boat far behind.

"We haven't exactly left her behind," the boat interrupts. "She just keeps stopping at all those islands to do a little beachcombing while we catch up."

"Well, we're ahead of her anyway. That's all that matters."

"Why, exactly, does that matter?" Jagular says.

Good question. I pretend not to hear him.

◆　　　◆　　　◆

My brother, who's sailing across from his own cottage farther up the inlet to join us, is even farther behind. He's just launching off the beach now, and I can barely see his sail, far across the bay. He's sailing a new boat he just finished building a few weeks ago, a lean streamlined cruiser with a gleaming white hull, lapstrake planking, and varnished decks. It's an elegant boat, a real beauty. A Ferrari to Jagular's battered Model T.

Jagular, though, has a certain charm. I like to think he's a bit like me: not flashy, not elegant, but maybe a little more capable than he appears. It's nice to see we're going to arrive at the beach first. That doesn't happen often.

"We were already more than halfway across the bay before your brother even hoisted his sail," Jagular points out. "And he's not that far behind anymore."

"So?"

"Just a random observation," he says.

◆   ◆   ◆

The rest of the family drove to the beach instead of spending the morning sailing across the hot and mostly windless bay. By the time we arrive, they've been there for hours. The picnic is over. All that's left is a chaotic jumble of nieces and nephews laughing and splashing around in the sandy shallows. The adults are all reading books, or watching the kids splash around, or napping, or playing with the kids, or lying in the sun, or settling disputes between kids, or trying to get the kids to eat something besides chocolate chip cookies, or asking some of the kids to share their goggles with some of the other kids who forgot theirs, or lost them, or broke them, or asking the kids "How many of those have you had already?" when they want more cookies, or settling more disputes between kids, or whatever.

To be honest, I'm not really paying that much attention. Life ashore is boring. I've only been here ten minutes and already I'm eager to continue sailing.

"Let's go," I tell Jagular.

"We're leaving so soon?" he says.

"Yes," I say. "We'll press on to Harbor Island—seas to be crossed, dangers to be faced, adventures to be had, life to be lived, all that sort of thing. We can't waste our time playing around at the beach with a bunch of kids."

"Trying for Uncle of the Year again, aren't you?" the boat asks. But he can't complain too much, because I'm not the only one; my brother has managed to arrange things so he can come along, too.

"In his fancypants lapstrake boat," Jagular says, watching me tie a reef in the sail. It's getting windier.

"Just be quiet and help me get ready," I say. "It always takes him a while to get going. We'll get a good head start."

"We'll need it," says Jagular.

◆   ◆   ◆

The water stays shallow for quite a ways off the beach, so I drag Jagular out a hundred yards where it looks like it might be deep enough to put the rudder down. It's getting pretty windy, a fierce northerly blowing straight toward shore. I'll have to think things through carefully before hoisting the sail. Once it's up, we won't have much time to get moving before the wind pushes us right back into the shallows. Leeboards, rudder, halyard, downhaul; there's a lot of stuff that has to happen all at once when you're launching a little boat in a lot of wind. It can get messy. But the hell with it, I decide. It's not rocket science. I scramble aboard, immediately tangling myself in the mainsheet.

"I kind of assumed that 'think things through carefully' meant you were going to keep thinking until you figured it all out," Jagular says.

"He who hesitates is lost," I tell him.

We've already been pushed a few yards back into the shallows, so I grab the halyard and start hoisting the sail, which blusters around in the wind, trying to wrap itself around me. And somehow the bow has fallen off to the wrong side, which means I'm hoisting the sail on the port tack instead of the starboard tack as I intended. We're headed east toward the shore's northward curve instead of west out into the open bay. Even worse, now that I've hoisted the sail halfway up the mast, it's doing its best to shove me overboard.

I duck back under the sail hurriedly, putting the whole flailing mess between me and the halyard, which is on the starboard side of the mast. As I'm trying to figure out how I'm going to finish hoisting the sail when I can't even reach the halyard, the sheet wraps itself around the tiller and the boom winds up and thumps me across the ribs repeatedly.

I give a couple of half-hearted tugs on the halyard, but the sail doesn't move—it's catching too much wind to slide any farther up the mast. I reach blindly under the sail and cleat the halyard off where it is, then grab the tiller.

The sail is partway up and halfway tangled up all over the cockpit in the way of everything, but there's so much wind that we're already sailing anyway. In the wrong direction, on a half-assed beam reach. There's no way we can make any distance to windward until I get the sail up, and no way to get the sail up until I get the boat pointed into the wind. All we can do is get shoved along clumsily toward shore. In about thirty seconds we'll be aground.

"Good thing you didn't hesitate," Jagular says.

Instead of answering him, I duck to the leeward side of the sail again, grab the halyard, and try hoisting the sail further up the mast again—*really* try this time. It still won't budge. The full force of the wind is pushing against the sail, locking it in place, and the full force of the sail is now pushing against me. Pushing me overboard, off the starboard side of the boat, where my weight is beginning to tip the boat over.

"I've never seen it done like that before," Jagular says.

"Shut up," I tell him, trying to duck back under the sail.

Everything is a mess. The sail is still only halfway up the mast. We're blundering along straight toward shore. I'll have to tack—that'll swing the sail to the port side of the boat and let me reach the halyard. I grab the tiller and steer us into the wind.

"Tacking," I tell Jagular.

"I doubt it," he says. "You haven't put the leeboard down yet. Or the rudder."

I drop the tiller and mainsheet and grab the oars.

"Tacking," I say again, gritting my teeth and pulling hard on the starboard oar.

"I wouldn't bet on it," Jagular says.

He's right. The sheet has wrapped itself around a leeboard cleat, sheeting the sail in tightly. And with the sail powered up, it's way too windy for me to row us around onto a starboard tack.

"Gybing, then," I tell Jagular, and pull hard on the port oar, shoving the tiller to windward with one foot. "Gybing!"

This time, turning downwind, the wind is on our side, and the bow slowly swings around. But now the sheet unwraps itself and runs out rapidly, letting the sail out so far it's almost forward of the mast. I grab the end of the sheet just before it slides into the water, and try to pull the sail over onto the new tack. It's like trying to lift an anchor at first, but then the whole baggy mass of sail slams violently over to port as the wind catches it, almost knocking us over again. Somehow I manage to duck the boom. The leeward rail dips under, scooping a little water into the cockpit, but I don't care. We're on a starboard tack now. Kind of.

"You probably should've hoisted the sail before you got in the boat," Jagular says.

The boom swings around and thumps me in the head.

◆   ◆   ◆

Eventually I manage to get it all straightened out and we're sailing north toward Harbor Island. It's pretty windy, but it's not too bad with a reef tied in. We're able to point just high enough to make it in one tack. One long cold and bumpy port tack. But we're actually doing pretty well. We're sailing.

I'm always amazed at how simple all this sailing stuff is, really. Tiller, halyard, mainsheet, leeboard, sail—nothing complicated. And yet, with these tools I'm able to invoke a complex array of natural forces, forces far older than life itself. Forces so immensely powerful that they can't be resisted or contained despite our best efforts. Dams fail. Rivers overrun their banks. Winds and waves topple trees, buildings, whole cities. Yet the simplest boat, the simplest sailor, can direct these forces into smooth, silent, effortless motion. A bit of line. A cheap tarp and a mast to hang it from. A rudder to deflect forces that cannot be overpowered.

Maybe the real value of sailing lies here, in the way it turns us toward simplicity, toward humility, restoring a perspective our technologically fundamentalist world so arrogantly rejects. There's no mastering the forces sailors invoke. There's no conquering going on. There are only things you can do, and things you can't—especially in a boat like Jagular. Resistance is not only futile, it's often disastrous. And so sailors learn to practice a purposeful and subtly productive submission to the inevitable. Wind. Waves. Tides. Currents. We learn to follow the fault lines between forces, seeking the easiest paths, the most harmonious methodologies. We become suspicious of strain and struggle, because struggling tends toward breakage, and breakage toward catastrophe.

In sailing, the presence of undue strain signals a failure of harmony.

"Sounds like you're becoming a Taoist," Jagular says.

"Maybe I am."

"Not a very good one, though," the boat continues. "Remember that time on your brother's sloop? When the rudder kicked up and you didn't realize anything was wrong despite the sudden extreme strain on the tiller? And you just kept struggling blindly, sailing along until the rudder broke?"

"That was a long time ago," I tell him.

"Broke right in half," Jagular says. "Inch and a half thick, wasn't it?"

I shake my head. "It's no use," I tell Jagular. "I do have my failings, lots of them, but today? Today is for sunlight on wavetops and strong winds raging through the bay, a day to dare great things, a day to remember. Even you can't interfere with that."

"Want to bet?" Jagular says.

◆   ◆   ◆

We're still ahead of my brother as we sail into Harbor Island's outer harbor, where we're protected from the wind by a long finger of forest reaching into Potagannissing Bay. There are a couple of big boats anchored farther up the harbor, but otherwise there's nothing but hardwood forest and cloud-studded blue sky and rock-studded shoreline, and the play of sunlight on the leaves overhead. The water is green and waveless here in the harbor, and so clear that I can see the rocky bottom twenty feet down. It's a surprisingly sudden transition from violence to placidity, from cold and wet to warm and sunny. But it's a false peace, reflecting only the shape of the land and not the weather itself. Once we round the corner back into the bay we'll be right at it again.

A minute or two later my brother joins us. He's had a good ride—it really is a fast boat—and even though he sailed a much longer route to get here, he almost managed to catch us before we reached Harbor Island.

"And we had a head start, too," Jagular reminds me.

"It's not a race," I say. "And besides, we won."

We beach the boats and poke around the rocky fringe of the island for a while, but I don't want to wait too long before setting out again. The first two legs of the journey—cottage to beach, beach to Harbor Island—were short hops through mostly sheltered waters. Now we're facing a four-and-a-half mile stretch of sailing, across open water with a big fetch. We'll be fully exposed to the wind, which has swung around further to the northwest and seems to be getting a lot stronger. There are waves now. Whitecaps. And there'll be nothing between us and Canada but a few small islands scattered about the bay.

"Four and a half miles is a long way in this wind," Jagular says.

"Yep," I agree.

"And we're still going?"

"Of course," I tell the boat. "Seas to be crossed, dangers to be faced—did you think I was making all that stuff up?

"Hope springs eternal," Jagular says.

◆   ◆   ◆

We set out from Harbor Island together, but my brother leaves us behind pretty quickly, heading southwest toward the tip of Gull Island. Jagular and I do our best to follow, but it's getting stupidly windy now. Big waves. Cold spray. Constant bailing. Hiking out. Heading up into the gusts, steering carefully to take the steeper and meaner waves at a gentler angle. I'm a little surprised to see that we're holding our course fairly well, though. The balance lug seems to be a big improvement over the spritsail. Way up ahead I can just see the sail of my brother's boat, and I even catch sight of the elegant white hull every now and then, when we both hit the crest of a wave at the same moment. We're doing all right. That could change in less than a moment, but for now we're all right.

Soon, though; soon we'll be sailing past the tip of Gull Island out into the open, into the huge mass of subarctic air being funneled southeastward down the St. Mary's River into Potagannissing Bay. It'll be rougher out there. And it doesn't seem like we can take much more than we're already taking.

"This could get interesting," I tell the boat.

"It usually does," he says.

◆   ◆   ◆

It's windy enough that I should probably be a little worried, but we're having too much fun. It's too ridiculous, what we're seeing out here today, beyond anything we've ever sailed in. The wind is a wall, an immense weight pushing hard against everything it touches. Even hiked out as far as I can get—my toes are hooked under the leeward side deck— the leeward gunwale rides low in the water. The waves are steep and close together, and when we hit one wrong, the lee rail ducks under and scoops up a bunch of the bay.

We're probably not going to make it, I realize, but the thought is exhilarating rather than frightening. Every moment we stay on our feet is unexpected. Pure unearned unadulterated grace. It's all I can do to hold the sheet; I've got it wrapped several times around the tiller so I can hold both with one hand, but the line keeps slipping and I have to adjust my grip every few seconds. Meanwhile I have to be bailing or we won't stay up much longer. But every time I lean over for another scoop of water we're in danger of capsizing anyway.

I wonder how it'll happen. A gust I can't compensate for? The rail going under and just not coming back up, letting the water roll us over slowly and gracefully? The sudden lurch of a big wave? A broken mast?

"My money's on pilot error," Jagular says.

"Mine, too," I say. "But it hasn't happened yet."

It may happen soon, though. I've been steering us as close to the wind as I can—not much higher than a beam reach

I'm a little surprised to see we're holding our course fairly well.

in this wind. But that heading has us a little to windward of where we should be. If we keep on, we'll miss the entrance to our cottage's inlet by sailing up the wrong side of Fairbank Point. I'm going to have to turn us downwind, onto a run instead of a reach.

"This'll be good," Jagular says.

In heavy winds and waves, downwind sailing invites disaster. A small flat-bottomed boat like Jagular will surf much like a surfboard. There'll be a sudden rush of exhilarating speed as the wave slides by beneath you, lifting you, launching you forward. You may double your speed while it lasts. But at any moment the bow could slide off to either side, turning you broadside to the waves, rolling you past recovery. The waves you were surfing a moment ago can start breaking into the cockpit. There's a good chance the boat will capsize. You're always at the edge of control, or maybe a little past it.

"Hell with it," I say. "Here goes." I nudge the tiller, turning us off the wind. We take off immediately on a wild ride through the waves, a rollickingly abandoned galloping plunging surfing rolling mindless exhilaration of speed and instability. I thought we were moving fast before but we

Weren't.

Even.

Close.

The boat is heeled over so far I'm practically standing on the leeward gunwale now, my body leaning way out over the side deck, trying to keep as much weight to windward as I can. It's not enough. The lee rail is slicing through the water completely submerged, only the narrow side deck keeping us from filling up completely.

I steer off the wind a bit more, hoping it'll be enough to keep us upright. The entire boat is humming loudly, and we're sailing faster than we've ever gone before. We're going much faster than a boat like Jagular was ever meant to go, we're flouting the rules of physics, throwing up our hands and leaving everything to chance, to Fate, to whatever forces may be paying attention. It's not defiance, it's pure submission. We'll either make it or not. Probably not.

Either way, it won't be up to us.

·   ·   ·

Three and a half miles later we sail into the lee of Fairbank Point. Again a long finger of land juts out into the bay, cutting off the wind and leaving us nearly becalmed. Far ahead of us, at the head of the inlet, my brother is just pulling his boat up on shore. We're alone again, Jagular and I. We've made it.

I slowly unclench my hand from the sheet and slide off the side deck. The cockpit is about one-third full of water. I look around: mast, rudder, tiller, leeboards, nothing seems to be broken. I start bailing. I bail for a long time, and sponge out the last puddles until the cockpit is dry. Then I take off my shirt and wring it out overboard, put it back on a little drier—but not much.

"Hell of a ride," I say. "For a while there I didn't think we were going to make it."

"I never think we're going to make it," Jagular says. "That way I end up with an occasional pleasant surprise."

"*Et tu, Brute?*" I say, and keep working, straightening up the cockpit, re-stowing the oars and float cushions, tucking the bailer and sponge under the side deck. We haven't even lost anything.

It's a nice evening all of a sudden. We've dropped from a gentle breeze to a faint one. Even the random gusts have died down. I think about rowing but decide not to. We'll get there eventually. And eventually is always soon enough.

I lean back against the aft bulkhead of the cockpit and smile as the boat moves slowly through the water. The tiller rests on my shoulder. The sheet is tied off to the leeboard cleat. All around us sunlight scatters sharp-edged sparks across the bay, and somewhere on shore children are laughing and shouting. The faint sound of a breeze shuffling through the trees, the slap of tiny waves against the hull. A perfect day. We have been weighed in the balance and have not been found wanting.

"This time, anyway," Jagular says. I shake my head and smile again.

After a while the cottage comes in sight up ahead, the long dock and the sandy beach wrapped in slowly growing shadows. The wind has dropped to almost nothing now, and we ghost along in silence. The sun drops behind the trees, just a thin glowing arc visible above Fairbank Point, hanging over the treetops like the edge of a sickle. What's left of the light glitters faintly on the water as the world begins to turn from gold to gray. Overhead the first stars appear in the darkening sky. We're almost home.

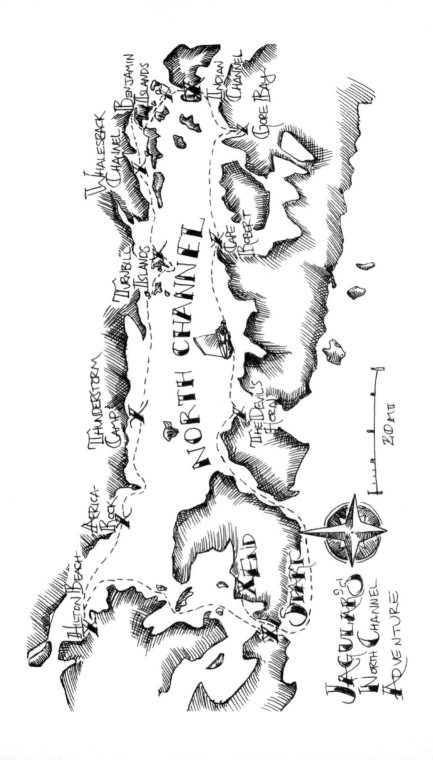

Whalesback Channel
Benjamin Islands
Indian Channel
Gore Bay
Turnbull Islands
Cape Robert
Thunderstorm Camp
Africa Rock
Hilton Beach
The Devils Elbow
START
NORTH CHANNEL
20 mi
Jaguar's North Channel Adventure

Jagular's
North Channel
Adventure

Shipwrecked

"Spring is here," I tell the boat as I pull the trailer out of the carriage house. "Time to start planning our summer cruise. I want to do something really big this year."

"Trying to get out of helping your brother re-roof his house?" Jagular asks.

"No," I tell him, then stop for a moment to pick up the carriage house door from where it has fallen into the mud. I lean it carefully back up against the door frame and hastily step away. "Well, yes, actually. But also, I'm not sure how much longer you're going to last."

"Whose fault is that?"

"Well, it's too late to do anything about that. But if we're going to do something big, we better do it soon. Listen to this." I pull out my copy of *Well Favored Passage*, Marjorie Cahn Brazer's classic guide to the North Channel, and start reading. "*To the mapmaker at a drawing board, the North Channel is a deep water passage between the Manitoulin Islands and the Ontario mainland at the northern extremity of Lake Huron.*"

"So?" Jagular says.

"Keep listening," I say. "*But to the mariner in a small boat it is far more than a place to be located by mathematically derived grids on a cold sheet of paper. To him it is a state of mind.*"

"So is insanity," the boat mutters. I ignore him and keep reading.

"*It is a flight of the soul to a distant haunt—of peace, of timelessness, of mystery, of tempest, of aching beauty. Its very name evokes a mood, an ephemeral feeling—recall for those fortunate enough to have been there, yearning for those who have only heard tell.*"

"And pity for those who have to go there with someone like you," Jagular says. "That's how I would have written it."

"You be quiet," I tell him. "Look, I've got the charts already. We'll start here, in De Tour Village—" I jab my finger down at the eastern edge of Michigan's Upper Peninsula— "and sail north to Canada, then east along the Ontario shore, through the Whalesback Channel, and all the way down to the Benjamin Islands." I poke a swirling bunch of islands somewhere west of Little Current. "Here."

"And then?"

"Who knows? Maybe you'll fall apart along the way and I'll take a bus back home. Maybe we'll keep going right off the chart and on into Georgian Bay. Or we could swing back to the west and make a loop of it. Sail back into the same harbor we started from, only wiser, and more experienced. With a better tan."

"I see you've planned this with your usual thoroughness," Jagular says.

"I did make a new sail," I tell the boat, unrolling the balance lugsail my brother and I put together over the weekend from a plastic tarp and carpet tape. "See? Easy to handle, easy to reef—not like that spritsail we had down in Texas."

"I'll withhold judgment for now," the boat says, eyeing the sail skeptically. "What about the leaky butt joint in the cockpit floor?"

I hold up a saw, a cordless screwdriver, a thick plank of Douglas-fir, and a strip of fiberglass cloth. "I'm going to fix that right now," I tell him. "Just let me mix a quick batch of epoxy and we'll be ready to roll."

There's a long silence.

"What?" I say. "Would you rather I started with the new mast step?"

Behind me the carriage house door falls to the ground with a soggy thud.

◆   ◆   ◆

But somehow everything gets done, and by the middle of July we're pulling in to De Tour Village, the western gateway to the North Channel. I launch Jagular at the municipal marina, park the car, load the gear and groceries, and row around to a quiet backwater of the harbor, where I tie off to a scraggly tree and scramble awkwardly ashore through the branches. Then I'm off to a local boatyard, where a greasy-fingered mechanic with an unruly mustache agrees to let me park the car and trailer for the next several weeks, in recognition of our common bond as sailors and boatmen. That, and sixty dollars in cash, no receipt. The brotherhood of the sea.

"And leave the keys," he says as I start to walk away. I hand them over and take a last look at my car. These days it's more temporary than the boat. The only thing I'll miss if the mustache takes it to a chop shop while I'm gone will be the Jimmy Buffet CDs under the front seat.

It's a two-mile walk back to the harbor. By the time I get there I'm half hoping someone has stolen the boat, forcing me to abandon my cruise. We're ready enough—new mast step, new sail, new oarlocks, new tiller, new rowing thwart— but it's a gray rainy day filled with blustery wind. Out in De Tour Passage the dark waters of Lake Huron are stirred into a checkerboard of whitecaps. Eighty-foot ferries and thousand-foot ore carriers motor up and down the narrow channel, leaving little room for small boat crossings at two or three miles an hour. And it's already late afternoon. Ten miles to sail before we reach Harbor Island to the northeast, the nearest land that's not privately owned. We might be able to camp there—illegally, most likely—hidden in the tall grasses along the shore. But who knows, really? By the time we get there it might be so dark I won't even be able to find the island, much less the harbor.

And it's windy as hell, a fierce northerly blowing straight down De Tour Passage. Not exactly how I wanted this all to begin. So I feel a faint hint of disappointment when I get back to the marina and find Jagular still tucked away safely under his tree. I climb aboard just as it starts to rain.

"That's it," I tell the boat. "Nothing much more can go wrong. Let's go."

The cockpit is crammed full of gear, but I don't feel like taking time to pack it away while it's raining. Instead I pile it into the corners where it's mostly out of my way, then pull out my secret weapon: a one-piece imitation Gore-Tex drysuit with built-in feet and waterproof rubber gaskets at the wrists.

"What's that?" Jagular asks.

"My get out of jail free card," I tell him, struggling to climb into the suit through the chest zipper, trying to twist my arms into the sleeves. "Now I can abandon ship with impunity."

"Assuming you can actually figure out how to wear it," Jagular says. "Are you supposed to put both arms in the same sleeve like that?"

I ignore him, too busy fighting the zipper to bother with a reply. It would help if I could dislocate at least one shoulder. But finally I'm in. The suit is zipped. No matter what happens, I'm going to be dry. "Let's hit it," I tell the boat, and row out into the harbor.

It's windy—too windy, really—but I'm not turning back now. I pull alongside the visitor dock to tie a reef in the new lugsail, though—I don't really know how, but I cobble something together that looks like it might work—then shove off again and row out through a break in the sea wall.

"Here we go," I say, stowing the oars. Then I hoist the sail, tie off the halyard, tighten the downhaul, and sheet in. I've even remembered to tie the boom parrel before hoisting so the sail doesn't kite away crazily in the wind. Anyone watching might assume I know what I'm doing. But no one is watching. Still, we're on our way, sailing a close reach east-northeast across De Tour Channel toward Harbor Island. Ten miles to go.

✦   ✦   ✦

It's windy, all right, with a steep chop and lots of cold spray. In our first hour of sailing we've already had to dodge two huge ore carriers, cutting back to the west side of the channel both times so we won't be run down, but this looks like our shot. There's no traffic in sight. I take us off the wind a bit so we can cross the channel more quickly. In a little over an hour we should be across.

"Don't worry about traffic," I tell Jagular as we bash our way through another set of waves. The dry suit is doing its job—I'm dry. The gear floating around the cockpit—my clothes, mostly, halfheartedly wrapped in unsealed trash bags—isn't. Too late to do anything about that, though. I'm hiked out on the side deck trying to keep us upright, and wishing I were back ashore. Wishing I had put another set of reef points in the sail. Wishing it weren't raining. But we're almost across the shipping channel, anyway.

"We're doing all right so far, so don't worry about the wind," I tell the boat. "Or the waves. This is what we're here for, after all. It's supposed to be an adventure, not a ladies' garden party."

"I like garden parties," he says.

And then before I can reply, the rudder pops off the transom and the wind turns us broadside to the steep waves and we've gone from mild discomfort to utter chaos in less than a second, the boat wallowing and threatening to go over, one oar popping off its socket and falling overboard, the rudder hanging from a single pintle, the tiller banging back and forth against the hull. I lunge forward to uncleat the halyard, drop the sail, yard, and boom into a sprawling mess all over the cockpit, and grab the tiller with one hand while I reach for the wayward oar with the other. A couple of waves have broken into the cockpit and the weight of the sloshing water is throwing the boat back and forth in ever-increasing arcs. My clothes have escaped the trash bags I packed them in and are floating all over the cockpit, getting in the way of everything. The anchor line for the cheap anchor I've borrowed from my brother wraps itself around my feet. Waves are breaking over the side decks.

I manage to keep hold of the tiller, but the lost oar is drifting away downwind, just out of reach. For a moment I contemplate a desperately heroic sideways grab to leeward to reach it. Then I contemplate the likely consequences and decide to hell with it. I haul the rudder aboard and start bailing instead. The wayward oar bobs along, and before long it's lost in the tumbling waves.

"Too bad you never installed that hold-down spring, huh?" Jagular says. "The one that's supposed to keep the rudder from popping off the mounting hardware like that?"

"At least we're drifting toward shore and out of the shipping lane," I tell him. "Things could get a lot worse than this."

"That's what I'm afraid of."

◆   ◆   ◆

The first landfall of our North Channel cruise: we've washed ashore on the northwest tip of Michigan's Drummond Island, a half mile south of Dix Point. Shipwreck Camp, I name it, dragging Jagular as far up onto the rocks as I can. The rain has stopped and the sky is clearing. I feel like Robinson Crusoe as I start salvaging everything I can from my unfortunate ship, spreading it out on rocks to dry. I look around for naked footprints in the sand but don't find any. Too bad. We've come about three miles from our launch point in De Tour Village, though. Far enough.

"We've made the essential break from civilization, anyway," I tell Jagular. "We'll regroup and set out again tomorrow. Head north for Canada."

"With one oar," the boat says. "And what's this about an essential break from civilization? Isn't that a house right over there? I bet we're not even supposed to be here."

He's right, there's a house about a quarter mile south along the shore, tucked way back among the trees. But if I stand in the right place, behind the scraggly stand of spruce that lines the shore where we landed, I can't see it. Good enough for me. I rig clotheslines all over the trees and hang everything up to dry. Then I set up the tent and start walking down the shore to think things over. We can probably make it to Hilton Beach without an oar. That's where I'm planning to clear Canadian customs anyway. It's only twenty miles away. The marina store there probably sells oars.

If there is a marina store. Can't go back, though. *Forward!*—it's the Wisconsin motto. Maybe Drummond Island Yacht Haven, just six or seven miles east, sells oars. I'm considering my options as I keep walking along, heading toward the line of houses tucked back on a low ridge above the channel. They look nice enough—cathedral-ceilinged prows, big windows, private docks, lakeshore patios and fire pits surrounded by teak furniture—but there's an air of abandonment about them, like a set of expensive toys left scattered around the yard. Weekend homes.

I can't imagine ever wanting a second house—it'd be like wanting a second disease. But I've reached the end of the uninhabited stretch now, and there's nothing but empty vacation homes and cabins and cottages from here, one after another, heading south along the water's edge as far as I can see. I'm about to turn back when I notice something else: the oar. My lost oar has been driven up onto shore handle-first, the blade bobbing in the shallows. I've been secretly hoping I'd run into it, and here it is. I run back to camp with the oar, laughing.

"Look, I found the oar!" I shout. "I found it!"

"God loves children and fools," Jagular says.

◆   ◆   ◆

Day two, gear mostly dry and stowed, ready for launching. Yesterday's whitecaps and fierce winds are gone, and I'm anxious to put some miles in while the good conditions hold. My handheld VHF radio spits a long string of coded MAFOR numbers that's supposed to tell me something about the weather forecast.

"What's it say?" the boat asks.

"Beats me. I left the code book in the car," I tell him. "Let's go."

I drag Jagular off the rocky shore and hop in and we're off to Canada. I row out a ways and raise the sail.

Not much wind.

We drift around for a while. I get a good look at Potagannissing Bay just east of us, an intricate scattering of thickly forested islands and clear green water. Meanwhile the sail flops around overhead. I nudge the tiller back and forth occasionally. Sometimes I convince myself we're getting closer to Big Trout Island. Other times it looks farther away. That's what small boat sailing is, mostly. Finally I drop the sail, peel off my drysuit, and start rowing.

I row past Bow Island.

Little Trout Island.

Big Trout Island.

Bacon Island.

I keep rowing past Maple Island, where a man is rumbling around aboard a D9 Cat that's belching smoke and ripping down trees and tearing up dirt and spitting mud around. Getting ready to turn the whole island into a giant condominium, I suppose. Maybe a golf course. Must get rid of the trees, the guests won't be able to see the lake.

"I bite my thumb at you, sir," I shout as I row past.

"You're not biting your thumb," Jagular says.

"I'm rowing."

"If you really cared, you'd stop."

"If I really cared, I'd do a lot more than that," I tell the boat. "For starters, I wouldn't drive 400 miles to drag you to Lake Huron. Would you rather stay cooped up in the garage all summer?"

Silence.

I row past Long Island.

Butterfield Island.

Norris Island.

I've been rowing for almost six miles, I suddenly realize, and it's been great. Slow, but so what? I'm not in any hurry. The water is dead flat, no wind, and I even got the oarlocks to stop squeaking by rubbing them with a lump of wax I've brought along. Time for a break. I drag the boat up onto a boulder on the northwestern tip Norris Island and wander the rocky shore for a few minutes, hopping from boulder to boulder trying not to fall in. It'll be our last landfall in the U.S. for a long time; from here it's just a half mile to the Canadian border, which on my chart is marked by a dotted magenta line. In reality it's marked by nothing at all.

"What nonsense," I tell the boat, tracing my finger along the chart's dotted line. "Human borders are arbitrary and capricious, existing only to promote conflicting ideologies and rabid nationalism. Lines on maps. Never mind that those Canadian molecules over there are banging around into these U.S. molecules over here, rendering all division meaningless as far as the natural world is concerned. But that's not good enough for us. We must have borders!"

"Is there anything you don't object to?" the boat asks.

"Without borders, what excuse would we have to wage industrial-scale violence on each other?" I insist. "*Dulce et decorum est* and all that." I put away the chart and stare across Tenby Bay into Canada, past the invisible border. I feel like I should make more of our visit to Norris Island but can't figure out anything to do. Eventually I climb back over the rocks and into the boat, grab the oars and start rowing again.

♦   ♦   ♦

"If you haven't run aground, you haven't been to the North Channel," I explain as I drag Jagular off the boulders that line the rocky tip of Richmond Point, just a couple of miles north of Norris Island. I've managed to row into these rocks at full speed. Full speed when you're rowing is just a little over two miles per hour, but even so, it makes a remarkable *thunk*. I'm keeping an eye out for the RCMP, since running aground in Canada is technically illegal until you've cleared Customs. We're on the wrong side of the magenta line now.

As I'm trying to hop back into the boat and shove us off, I slip off the slimy rocks into waist-deep water and barely manage to scramble back aboard. Cold water. It's raining now, too, so I pause to pull on my drysuit and start rowing again.

I row past Salt Island.

Beef Island.

Hog Island.

It's raining harder now, with the first faint stirrings of a breeze. Halfway past Hog Island, after twelve or thirteen miles of rowing, the breeze grows to a good southerly wind, and I finally raise the sail. Soon we're really moving, a quick broad reach up the east shore of St. Joseph Island to Hilton Beach—the new balance lug rig is turning out to be fast off the wind. It's cold, though; cold in a wet drizzly kind of way that has me thinking fondly of heat in all its many forms. I imagine climbing into the warmth of a car that's been parked in the sun on a hot day. I think about fires. Stoves. Hot tubs. Molecules banging into each other. But apparently the invisible border has put a stop to that kind of fraternization after all.

And wearing a drysuit without insulation underneath is like wearing a frogskin, I'm finding out: obscenely clammy and not especially warm. I'm starting to shiver now that I'm not rowing. I'd like to pull on my fleece top for more insulation, but shedding a drysuit in a small open boat while sailing would require contortionist abilities that I don't have. I'd probably end up in the water watching Jagular sail away northward.

"You'd be glad to get rid of me, wouldn't you?" I ask. "I bet you're just waiting to give me the deep six."

No answer.

◆   ◆   ◆

Up here on the eastern shore of St. Joseph Island, the forest crowds close to the shore, leaving narrow rocky fringes at the lake's edge. No buildings or roads in sight. The North Channel. One of the places you're supposed to sail before you die, I've read. Not that you have to die as soon as you sail here, I remind whoever is listening—just in case someone is.

After a while I start to see a few other sailboats, big fiber-glass sloops motoring northward farther offshore. Sailboats motoring north, with a southerly wind. Crews hiding out in pilot houses, behind dodgers, below decks, even. They're motoring because those kinds of fat-bodied sloops wallow like epileptic hogs when sailing downwind, but that's no excuse as far as I'm concerned. "It's a sailboat! Not a motorboat!" I shout at each one as it passes. None of them answer. Probably none of them even know we're here.

"They're going to be sitting around for hours, all warm and dry and comfy, before we even come in sight of wherever it is we're going to camp," Jagular says. "You know that, right?"

"They're warm and dry right now, the bastards," I tell him. "They're all sitting around in their fancy salons playing pinochle and drinking rum, letting the autopilot and the GPS handle the navigating."

Still, we're moving well by Jagular standards, almost a fast walking pace. Soon we're past Caradoc Point, and on past Big Point, and almost to Brickyard Bay, where I was planning to stop for the night. I'm very cold now, shivering so much it's hard to hold the tiller steady, but it's early in the day. And the wind is still good.

Hell with it, I decide, and cut straight across the open water far from shore, heading toward Gravel Point instead of into Brickyard Bay. Hilton Beach is only seven or eight miles further.

Somewhere in my cold-fogged mind is a sluggish awareness that I may be growing mildly hypothermic, though— reflexes slowing, attention wandering, making stupid mistakes; sailing dead across the wind with the sail eased way out, for instance, as if we're still running downwind. Eventually I realize our new heading has put us on a beam reach, and sheet in tightly. Jagular surges forward, moving fast enough—especially this far offshore— to be a little scary. But if we can make it around the corner we'll have it made.

I'm thinking of the hot shower that's waiting for me if we can just make it to a Hilton Beach hotel room.

"Do you even know if Hilton Beach has a hotel?" Jagular asks.

"Of course not. That's why it's an adventure," I tell him. "Because we don't know anything."

There's a moment of silence before the boat replies. "You must have a lot of adventures."

◆　　　◆　　　◆

Day three. Hilton Beach has a hotel, thank God, and the woman at the desk—after eyeing me for a long moment without comment—agreed to let me have a room. Cash only. After a long and luxuriously hot shower, I finally stopped shivering, then went out to hunt down something for supper. Hilton Beach, it turns out, has two restaurants: one for locals, one for tourists. The bartender at the tourist place fried me some mushrooms and onion rings last night to take back to my room—better than nothing. For breakfast I head to the local joint, where there's a well-worn sign behind the counter:

> You Have Two Choices:
> 1) Take it
> or
> 2) Leave it

Which sums things up pretty nicely, I think. I take it, and sit near a table full of farmers in overalls and greasy ball caps while I eat, wondering what they'd make of my trip. Unlike me, they've been shaped by years of hard work and relentless knucklebusting practicality. Dairy farmers don't take many vacations, not with twice-a-day milking. I can't decide whether to envy them for their strength of character, their apparent willingness to be content with a life of hard work, or pity them for the limits I imagine a life like that imposes—not just on your time, but on the very structure of your thoughts, your priorities, your willingness to dream big wild stupidly impractical dreams.

These farmers don't seem worried about any of that, though. They're talking about the weather. Will it be another wet summer? How many hay crops will they get in? Honest unpretentious talk that's firmly rooted in the practical, the utilitarian. Instead of 'there' and 'that,' they say 'dere' and 'dat,' which makes me feel right at home—I could be in a diner in northern Wisconsin. But a slow series of rising and falling inflections sweeps through their sentences almost at random, as if each phrase has to be eased along a line of gently rolling hills, and many sentences end with a rhetorical 'eh?', making their speech seem like almost a parody of a Canadian accent. I'll get used to that, I suppose. By the end of the week I'll probably be wearing a toque and thinking in metric. I spend a moment trying to convert knots to kilometers but give up almost immediately. I'm not even sure how to manage the conversion between knots and miles per hour. And besides, we've really only got one speed: slow.

After breakfast I wander the streets of Hilton Beach—both of them—for a while. There's a big cultural event in town every summer, an art fair and music festival that features artists and performers from all over St. Joseph Island and mainland Ontario. Brings the whole town to life. The biggest tourist draw on the whole island. There are posters for it everywhere: gas stations, telephone poles, store windows. It was yesterday.

I finally give up and head back to the boat. Down at the marina, Jagular waits alone at the transient dock, lost among the big sloops and powerboats, looking seedy and decrepit among all the chrome and white paint. Transient. I roll the word around on my tongue, enjoying its subversively bohemian allusions, its promise of freedom from routine and convention. Then I pile my gear on the dock for repacking, and kneel down beside the boat to start cramming stuff into the watertight storage compartment in Jagular's bow.

Canned ravioli. Canned lasagna. Ramen noodles. Lemonade mix. Granola bars. Poncho liner. Tent. More noodles. Stove. Clothes. Books. Spare batteries for the VHF. Spare batteries for the camera. More clothes. More books. Eventually everything is inside, the hatch tightly closed. All that's left out is a small day bag filled with snacks, a water bottle, a book or two, my drysuit, the chart, the anchor, two float cushions, a life jacket, my emergency packet with flares, whistle, and air horn, the handheld VHF radio, a folding knife, a waterproof flashlight, a spare water bottle, the bailer on its long leash, a—hell, there's a lot of junk still cluttering up the cockpit. I pretend to straighten it up neatly, but really I'm just shoving it all around to different places. Finally I give up.

Ready at last. I climb into the cockpit and cast off the dock lines. Just as I start rowing, a thirty-foot cabin cruiser motors up to the fuel dock, diesel engines rumbling, a halo of fumes hanging overhead. Yellow-shirted teenage dock workers materialize from all directions, catching heaving lines, adjusting fenders, talking on handheld radios, hooking up fuel lines and water hoses and electrical cables, politely pretending to listen to the captain's advice while quietly and efficiently doing whatever they're supposed to be doing instead. That's the welcome you get if you're spending hundreds of dollars on fuel and slip fees.

It's different in a three-hundred-dollar sailboat. Last night exactly no one met us at the dock. We sailed silently past the entrance buoys, threaded our way through the narrow L-shaped approach channel, and spun about into the wind just as we reached the visitors' dock. A gentle bump and we were alongside, where I dropped the sail in a neat bundle. I imagined the people on the other boats watching secretively, be-grudgingly intimidated by the obvious ease and seamanship with which I handled it all, an ease borne of long practice and hard-won experience.

I think he sailed that little boat all the way from Michigan, I imagined them saying. *Now that's a real sailor! You wouldn't catch me going that far in a little boat like that*—all these remarks spoken in hushed voices and tones of reverent awe. But of course no one was watching. The other boats were all empty, languishing alone and untended in their slips.

After peeling off my drysuit, I called up Canadian cus-toms from the dockside courtesy phone to find out what I needed to do to enter the country.

"How long is your boat?" asked the woman who answered my call.

"Fourteen feet," I said. There was a muffled snort that might have been a chuckle.

"What make and model?"

"It's home-made," I said. The Customs agent laughed out loud, gave me a clearance number and wished me good luck, and I was officially ashore in a foreign land. The invis-ible magenta line was behind me. Kind of disappointing, actually. I was hoping someone would stamp my passport—*Arrival by Sea.* Still, the brief phone call served to reinforce certain romantic notions about what it means to be a sailor. I had become an international voyager. I was, technically, the master of a vessel, a self-directed wanderer using noth-ing but the power of the wind to propel me, following no schedule but that of wind and wave and weather, free to pursue my obsessions wherever they might lead me. Some-what consoled by these grand thoughts, I wrote my clear-ance number on a scrap of paper I carefully tucked away in my wallet, where it soon got wet and collapsed into a state of lumpy and sodden illegibility.

◆   ◆   ◆

We leave Hilton Beach just in time to avoid lunch ashore and head east, aiming for the main body of the North Channel a few miles ahead. We've turned the corner now, the northward leg of our journey over. For the next eighty miles we'll be paralleling the Ontario mainland, a rocky stretch of shoreline punctuated by a few towns that have evolved from wilderness to lumber camps to mining towns to their present obscurity. This stretch of coast is flat and featureless, but a string of islands just offshore provides makes it easy to keep track of where we are. And Jagular's compass shows us heading steadily toward E, which is right where we're supposed to be going.

When we round the corner of St. Joseph Island into the North Channel proper five or six miles from Hilton Beach, a walloping southerly wind meets us with a sudden ferocity: sailing around a corner means sailing into a different set of winds and waves and currents, which can be dangerous if you're not paying attention. We've gone from a downwind run in a gentle breeze to a close reach in more wind than we need. The boat is still thumping along, bashing its way through the waves, but it's a wet ride and we're rolling alarmingly. We'll have to reef the sail.

"This ought to be good," Jagular says.

I've read enough to know how to reef, in theory. I even tried it for real on our brief run across De Tour Channel two days ago, although I wasn't entirely happy with the result. But I'm hardly an expert sailor; I improve only by repeating and modifying various marginally effective behaviors I discover through trial and error. Like natural selection, it's a slow process. At least I put in a line of reefing points when I made the sail, though. That'll make it easier.

"I thought your brother made the sail," Jagular says.

"He helped."

"He helped?"

"All right, he made the sail, and *I* helped," I admit. "But I'm the one who put the reef points in."

"I thought so. They're supposed to be in a straight line, right?"

"Whatever. The important thing is that I put them in."

Even though the new lugsail is supposed to be easy to reef, though, I'll need to make some changes from my first attempt two days ago. It worked, kind of, but we ended up with a mess: the sheeting angles all wrong, the downhaul too far back, the yard hoisted too far forward. I'll need to re-attach the sheet to the boom by running the sheet through a different reef point grommet this time—but which one? And where should I re-tie the downhaul? And will I need to find a new place to cleat the sheet? I might need to adjust the halyard, too, move the attachment point further back-ward or forward on the yard. And how to make a neat and tidy job of it all so I don't end up with a wildly flapping and flogging mess?

"Most people would've figured all that out before launch-ing," Jagular says.

"Look around," I say. "Do you see any of these 'most peo-ple' around?" Silence. "No," I answer for him. "You don't. Because those 'most people' are so overcautious that they never end up doing anything. Sure, they set up their boat in the driveway and figure out how to reef everything all neat and tidy—but then the boat just sits there in the driveway! They never do anything!"

"You're the only one who ever goes sailing," Jagular says.

"Look around! Do you see anyone else?"

"The only one."

Before I can answer, a fierce gust hits and I have to head up into the wind and scramble for the side deck to keep us upright. By the time the crisis passes I've forgotten what I was going to say, so I just keep sailing. With luck we'll make it to shore where I can figure all this out— that'll be a lot easier than trying to wrestle the sail around in these waves, with the boat doing its best to throw me overboard. There's an island just a couple of miles away, right on our heading. We'll probably make it.

◆   ◆   ◆

"Cedar Island," I tell the boat when we finally arrive safely ashore. Like most of the islands we've seen so far, it's a thick tangle of mixed pines and hardwoods, interrupted here and there by rocky slabs and boulders. "This is where twelve-year-old Ken McColman and his sister washed ashore in a storm after one of their boat's oars snapped. This was back in 1936. November. They were stranded for three days, with no food or shelter. Cold. Stormy. Wet. They finally gave up on being rescued, got in their one-oared boat and rode a southerly wind back to the mainland, then hitch-hiked twenty miles back home."

"So?" Jagular says.

"So, this kid's twelve years old, and he's out rowing around the North Channel in an open boat with his little sister, gets into trouble, and rescues himself. For fun!"

No answer. "Look," I say, "when's the last time you saw a twelve-year-old do anything like that? Today's kids spend all their times playing computer games and watching TV and sitting around not having adventures. They never even step outside."

"Why are you so cranky all the time?" Jagular asks.

"Because the world demands it of me," I say. "Forget *Forward!* as an official motto. *Convenience super omnia,* that's what it should be. Forget adventure: just get me a bag of chips, an iPhone, a TV remote, and get out of the way."

"You're eating a bag of chips right now."

"Sun Chips, though. That's practically health food."

◆   ◆   ◆

By sunset things have calmed down and I've shaken out the reef I tied in at Cedar Island. Reefing wasn't so bad this time. I even figured out a better way to rig the mainsheet, using the leeboard cleat on the side deck instead of the ring lashed to the rudder head. The rudder will never pop off the transom again. In theory.

Now we're bobbing along in a light wind about four miles west of Thessalon Point, where I'd hoped to camp. There's enough wind to sail, but a big leftover swell from the southeast won't let us make any headway, slamming the boat to a stop every time we get moving. The sail slaps back and forth, the boom thumps my head repeatedly, the boat stumbles and rolls, and we're not making any progress.

"Just stop waving!" I shout at the water. "You're doing it wrong. That southeast thing was so yesterday!" Finally I give up and start rowing, and even that's hard. Passing Africa Rock (named for a steamer that was wrecked there, a portentous detail I neglect to mention to Jagular), I decide to quit for the day.

"We're stopping here?" Jagular asks. "On a rock?"

"We have to camp somewhere," I say. "And besides, it's a big rock. Plenty of room." Easy access, too; there's a good landing point on the leeward side, a slab of smooth granite that drops directly into the lake, angled gently enough to pull Jagular completely out of the water.

The gulls of Africa Rock are angry at our intrusion, though, and migrate to the other end of the island, grumbling and muttering, plotting mutiny. And there's a strange inhuman emptiness about Africa Rock, as if the stark and enduring geology of the place feels no need to acknowledge our

There's a strange inhuman emptiness about Africa Rock.

brief tenure as the planet's dominant species. The coarse granite is covered with long streaks of old bird droppings. A few desiccated gull carcasses with no eyeballs are scattered about the rock—eyeballs, apparently, are a particular delicacy. A few broken eggs. A couple of tightly clustered nest groupings pasted to the steep rock. More bird droppings. Feathers. Squadrons of gulls circle and squawk overhead, dragging long shadows across the waves.

At the northern edge of the rock I find a deer skeleton stretched across the gray stone, ribs curling skyward like cupped hands, the skull aiming an empty stare out over the waves. We're a couple of miles offshore and the rock is completely bare of vegetation, but here it is. And why not? It's no more out of place than I am, maybe. I continue my exploration. More bird droppings. Bird vomit, lots of it, in a wide range of colors and textures, long streaks of it spreading out like bony fingers clawing at the rock beneath. And the grumbling chorus of gulls is everywhere, eyeing me suspiciously, moving in slowly now and then, testing the limits of our fragile truce. To establish a more permanent territorial claim, I set up my tent on the only flat space available, a small gravel patch bedded in guano. It's very soft.

Finally there's nothing left to do, and I sit down to watch the light fade from the day. After three days I'm just beginning to feel like it might be possible to escape my cluttered life ashore, at least temporarily. Sailing—this kind of sailing, anyway—has a way of paring things down to a skeletal beauty, a simple awareness that leaves no room for distractions. There's nothing to do but immerse myself in the experience, become a participant in the events unfolding around me, the ceaseless small happenings that are so easy to ignore at other times.

I've set up my tent facing south, out into the wide open North Channel. The mainland is out of sight behind me.

Overhead the skies slowly fill with scattered clusters of stars. A lone cloud floats by like a ghostly exhalation from some unseen presence, and the only sound is the small slap of the waves against the shore and the occasional rustle of the gulls. I can just see Jagular pulled up onto the ledges at the southern edge of Africa Rock, then a long stretch of open water that seems suddenly bigger, lonelier, than I counted on when I began.

A Narrow Escape

MORNING BRINGS A GENTLE BREEZE and a few white clouds moving slowly through the sky like scattered sheep. The sun climbs slowly above the horizon and the rough granite of Africa Rock seems brighter than it did yesterday, the wide waters to the south calm and inviting. Moods are built of such small things: darkness and waves, morning sunlight and blue skies. Today even the gulls seem lively and bright as they wheel through the air above us.

But the deer skull at my feet seems to stare up at me as if it knows something I don't. I'm trying not to pay attention. For the next forty miles we'll be sailing along the rockbound coast that forms the northern edge of the North Channel. The chart shows clusters of asterisks and crosses and dots liberally sprinkled all along the shore, a long belt of markings that represent rocks—shoaling, half-submerged rocks that lie hidden among the waves like sets of jagged teeth. My copy of *Well-Favored Passage* describes this stretch of the North Channel as "*inadvisable for small boats without sufficient power to cruise at least ten to fifteen miles an hour.*" There it is, right on page twenty-three. *Inadvisable for small boats.* All along I've been secretly dreading this part of the journey, and now here we are. Without a plan, as usual.

"The ship was the pride of the American side…" Jagular sings softly, his voice trailing off into an ominous silence.

"You're not helping."

"We could head offshore and hop from island to island."

"Sure," I tell him. "Four miles south to Thessalon Island, then ten miles east to Bigsby, and another five to West Grant. Long stretches of open water with big fetches and God knows what kind of storms brewing up, just waiting to sock it to us when it's too late to turn back."

"Maybe. But I'd rather try the islands than those rocks," Jagular says.

"Well, I'm the captain, and I'd rather be close enough to shore that we can get to a beach if we need to. Besides, when did you get so daring, anyway?"

"Since you started wanting to do things that are so inadvisable," the boat mutters. "It's not your bottom that's going to get chewed up on those rocks on the way in."

"It might be," I tell him.

It's a beautiful day, though, and it won't do any good to wait around hoping that things won't get worse. Things always get worse eventually. It's just a question of how long we have until that happens. Time to get moving. I stow the tent aboard, snap a photo of Jagular in the bright sunlight, and then with a quick slide down Africa Rock's rocky ramp, we're launched and underway. I look at my watch, hanging from a strap under the starboard side deck. 7:02 a.m. I row out a few yards and hoist the sail.

Not much wind.

We drift around for a while as usual, trying to work our way southeast on a close reach. Overhead the sail flops lazily back and forth. I get a good long look at Africa Rock behind us. The gulls are squawking and fluttering above it, rising into the sky and diving back down as if the rock is a bloated carcass they've returned to feed on. Up ahead, three or four miles east, the long snout of Thessalon Point marks our progress. Sometimes it looks closer. Sometimes it looks farther away. Finally I take down the sail and start rowing.

Two and a half hours later we pull into the shallows just off Thessalon Point. When I check the chart I see that we've only come six or seven kilometers.

"That's not even five miles," I tell the boat, running through the conversion in my head. "At this rate we'll never make it."

"You should have rowed faster."

"Well, I've rowed enough, anyway," I say, and hoist the sail again. Slowly it spreads out and catches what little wind there is, a faint northeast breeze. I turn us to starboard and we're sailing, heading southward into the open water. I tie off the self-steering lines and let the tiller mind itself.

◆   ◆   ◆

For the next several hours we work our way through a series of long tacks in light winds. It's bad tactics, I know—we're likely to get caught way off course if the wind shifts—but short-tacking in this breeze, in this boat, would be an exercise in futility. And so I leave the self-steering in charge for five, ten, fifteen minutes at a time before shifting to the new tack and starting all over again. We're barely moving, but out here far from shore, with few reference marks, it's easier to ignore our lack of progress.

Every time we head south, on the port tack, the wide open North Channel lies ahead: Thessalon Island four miles out, then tiny Sulphur Island beyond, and way off at the horizon, a smudge of blue that must be Drummond Island back in Michigan. On the starboard tack, headed back to the northeast, it's the town of Thessalon, way off at the base of Thessalon Point. I can barely make out a tiny Canadian flag hanging above the marina. A couple of huge gravel piles stand over town on the east side, threatening to overrun the city and spill into the harbor—the sawmills of the nineteenth century have been replaced by the slag heaps of the twentieth. Makes me wonder what's going to be next.

I push the tiller to port and the bow swings south toward Sulphur Island and the open water beyond. Push the tiller to starboard and we're headed back toward Thessalon and its towering gravel piles.

Sulphur Island. Thessalon. Sulphur Island again. Thessalon.

"This is ridiculous," I tell the boat. "We're making so little progress that I could shake hands with myself at each tack if we could jump back in time half an hour to do it."

That would be nice, actually. I could tell myself to forget this sailing nonsense. Just head into Thessalon Harbor and spend the day eating pancakes at the marina restaurant, I'd say. Watch the gravel piles advancing slowly toward the city to bury everything in a heap of slaggy ruin. Then wander through the end of civilization looking for someone you can say *I told you so* to.

◆   ◆   ◆

The long slow slog to windward continues, making a mockery of the warning in *Well Favored Passage*. "This stretch of sailing is inadvisable, all right," I tell Jagular. "Not because it's dangerous. But if you can't hit fifteen miles an hour you might die of boredom."

Farther offshore a fat sloop motors by, heading west on the faint east wind, sails furled and sail covers on. A gray Zodiac hangs off the back of the cockpit like an overstuffed sausage that can't quite manage to climb all the way aboard. The crew is out of sight, hiding down below while the electronics handle the ship. A radar antenna swings slowly back and forth on the cabin top, the only sign of life.

"I have a new theory," I tell Jagular, sitting up to shift onto the starboard tack again. "The amount of sailing a boat does is inversely proportional to the amount of money it costs."

"Why are you so judgmental all the time?" the boat asks. "Your constant criticism reflects a pathologically misanthropic worldview."

"It's not misanthropic to notice that the more stuff we have, the more gadgets we surround ourselves with, the less we're able to do for ourselves. And the less we do, the unhappier we become. But it's human nature. Even though we know it's no good for us in the long run, we take the easy way out whenever we can."

"Which is why we're sailing right now when rowing would be twice as fast?" Jagular says.

"Exactly."

"And you're arguing that the more arduous the methods we employ to achieve our goals, the more satisfaction we derive from our efforts. And thus, the happier we become."

I stop to think for a moment. "I suppose."

"Then you should be rowing."

I look around. We're a long way offshore. It's hot. No shade.

"It's the only way to maximize your happiness," the boat points out.

"The hell with that," I tell him, slumping back against the side deck again. "I don't need maximum happiness. I'm after relative happiness."

"You just made that up."

"It makes perfect sense, though. It's the old bear country tactic—you don't have to outrun the bear, you just have to be faster than the people you're hiking with. We're sailing, and he's motoring. We're happier. We win."

"You can't both be happy?" Jagular says. "Someone has to lose so you can win?"

"That's how it works. Human society demands clearly defined winners and losers. *Ordnung ist alles*. Which is why I'd rather go cruising than racing—I like the freedom of sailing alone. No rules. No pressure to outperform anyone. No competition."

"I thought you didn't like racing because you never win," Jagular says.

"That, too," I admit.

The sloop disappears slowly into the distance and we wallow on listlessly, too unambitious to continue our conversation. But the wind slides farther and farther southward all afternoon. By late afternoon we're heading due east on a beam reach, paralleling the rocky lee shore about a mile off. It's getting windier, too, and our speed picks up considerably as the wind continues to build. Clouds are stacking up on the horizon behind us, and a few whitecaps are forming.

"Inadvisable for small boats," Jagular says.

I pull out the chart again, looking for somewhere to hide in case things get bad. Asterisk cross cross asterisk. Asterisk cross. Twenty-five miles of rocks yet. I ease the sheet and head off on a broad reach until we're sliding along past the shoaling, inhospitable coast at top speed. Four and a half miles an hour.

◆   ◆   ◆

By evening a ragged curtain of gray clouds has closed down across the western sky, bringing on an eerie green-gray twilight that feels like the shadow of something I'd rather not turn around to see. I fumble my way into my drysuit as the first fingers of lightning start to spark across the clouds behind us. The approaching storm rumbles along in a wall of gray thousands of feet high, gaining on us rapidly. The wind is really picking up and we're sailing fast and I should probably tie in a reef. Instead I sheet in and start to head closer to shore.

"You see those rocks, don't you?" Jagular asks.

I couldn't miss them if I wanted to. The entire shoreline is fringed with a reef of granite, just as the chart shows. Waves are breaking over the rocks and sending brief flashes of spray into the air. Overhead the clouds have almost reached us and the sky is dark. Lightning. Thunder. Waves. Rocks. Big black badass clouds now, rumbling and muttering overhead, a little rain. The waves are building, too. Lots of whitecaps. There's fifteen miles of open water off to starboard, plenty of room for big waves to get bigger.

"The hell with this," I tell the boat as lightning flashes overhead.

"The hell with that," he says as a wave smashes into a rock a few yards to port.

"That about sums it up," I agree. But we have to try something, and none of the choices seem particularly appealing. I steer toward land, where there's a strip of sandy beach along the shore. Rocks. Breaking waves. More rocks. I steer away. Lightning. Thunder. More lightning.

A half mile farther down the shore I head in toward another sandy beach, this one broad and inviting and clear of rocks—but out of nowhere there are people on the shore, wading in the shallows, walking barefoot in the sand. I can see them smiling, laughing, stopping to toss a pebble into the waves, pick up a bit of broken glass. The arrogance! Safe ashore, oblivious to the trouble we're in as the storm rages on around us. I steer away from shore again, preferring probable disaster to certain spectacle. Overhead the sky unleashes another guffawing peal of thunder.

We're in among a field of boulders now, and the waves are big enough to hide them deep in the troughs. I'm at the tiller, but I'm no longer in control. Now and then a bigger-than-average wave splashes into the cockpit, soaking everything aboard and unbalancing the boat even further as the water sloshes from side to side.

We've left the people and their sandy beach far behind, and now my failure to go ashore when I had the chance enrages me. We should have sailed right up onto the sand among them like a car crash and the hell with avoiding the spectacle. I check the zipper on my drysuit, tighten the neck seal. Rocks. Thunder. Lightning. Rain. More rain. Growing darkness and the wind still building strongly. Whitecaps everywhere, the waves too big to do anything but run off now. I really should stop to tie in a reef, but if I do the storm will catch us for sure. And with no mizzen to hold the bow into the wind, even dropping the sail might be more than I'd care to try in these conditions. We keep sailing along on a broad reach instead, paralleling the shore while the waves get bigger and more aggressive and somewhere above us in the clouds our fate is being decided.

Then out of nowhere a log rears up, leaping out of a wave crest and launching itself at us like a battering ram. It thumps the side of Jagular's hull and drops back into the water.

"The hell with this!" I shout, and swing the boat toward land again. There's a bit of a bay just ahead, with a tiny pocket of pebbly beach. A couple of run-down cottages stand on the shore above, but I'm not waiting for a better chance this time. The mass of clouds has caught us, hanging overhead like a dark fist raised for smiting, and the waves are walloping along all too enthusiastically. We can probably camp down close to the water without being seen.

"If we make it that far," Jagular mutters.

We're running dead downwind toward shore now, moving fast enough that any collisions would be disastrous. Rocks. Thunder. More rocks. Waves. Lightning. Rocks.

"Asterisk asterisk asterisk cross asterisk cross," calls the chart suddenly.

"Shut up," I say, steering through the breaking waves, heading right for the tiny pocket of beach.

"Asterisk asterisk," says the chart helpfully. "Depth one meter."

I swing the tiller to take us around another floating log. Too late, I realize the obvious: I should have dropped the sail a mile offshore and rowed in. That would have calmed everything down. Instead we're screaming toward shore on a dead run through a gauntlet of granite boulders. We're in shallow water even this far out, and every time we hit a trough the rudder drags across the bottom. And now I can see that the pocket of beach I've been aiming for is surrounded by rocks. There's no way we can sail up onto it.

"That's it," I announce. "You got me." As the next wave passes beneath us, I let the sheet fly. The sail slams out over the bow. I drop the tiller and roll out of the boat into the water like a drunk falling off a barstool. And then I'm standing in knee-deep water thirty yards offshore, and Jagular is bobbing quietly by my side in the waves, the sail weathervaning freely. Behind us lies a chaotic rumble of seething violence, waves smashing into rocks and surging skyward in bright bursts of spray, but we've made it through.

Overhead the sun breaks through the clouds and a rainbow appears in the eastern sky.

◆   ◆   ◆

There'll be no problems about camping here, anyway. The cottages I saw on our approach are abandoned, or at least unoccupied. A dirt road runs through the camp—a scattered assortment of sagging cabins and decaying trailers, with the usual trash and beer cans scattered around—and continues on into the forest where it's soon lost from view among the scraggly jack pines. *This is the Conlins' Camp*, a hand-lettered sign near the end of the road tells me. The end of the road. Somehow I thought it'd be harder to get to.

"It's all an illusion," I tell Jagular when I get back to the beach.

"What is?"

"This," I say, waving my arms. "Ontario. It looks like a wilderness, but Trans-Canada Highway 17 is only a few miles inland and the beaches are covered with tire tracks and the forests are full of beer cans and broken bottles. It's no use. We've come forty miles and gotten nowhere. There's no escape, no blank spaces left on the map. Everything's been explored, explained, and exploited. We've clear-cut and over-fished and mined everything, let the slag heaps overtake the cities, built cottages and summer homes on the last good bits, and given the rest back to the Indians." I hold up the chart. "We're somewhere near the Thessalon Indian Reserve, see? Probably on it."

"Great," the boat says. "Another white guy showing up uninvited."

Still, it's a relief to be ashore, invited or not. The run in through the rocks could have turned a lot uglier than it did. I stare out into the lake and watch waves breaking over the rocks scattered all up and down the shore, as far out into the lake as I can see. Stupid, stupid, stupid, I tell myself. Why didn't you just drop the rig and row in? What kind of idiot sails at full speed through a thunderstorm over three quarters of a mile of rocky shoals and breaking waves? I should be wading through the shallows right now picking up pieces of my boat. But my stupidity has gone unpunished again and there it is.

What kind of generals do you prefer? someone asked Napoleon once. Lucky ones, he supposedly answered. He'd have loved me.

But it's turning into a pleasant evening after all we've been through to get here. The storm has passed through rapidly, leaving clear skies and a clean silence here at the edge of the

North Channel's widest expanse. It's fifteen miles across to Cockburn Island and the southern shores of this inland sea. Dark-needled spruce and pine forests crowd the rocky peninsula, sheltering the run-down cottages and cabins, and there's no one else in sight, nothing to break the silence except the wind and waves.

As the sun drops toward the horizon and the rainbow fades from the sky, I set up the tent on the beach and wander through the camp again. Off at the edge of the woods I find a decrepit privy, the door hanging by one rusty hinge. Better than nothing, I decide, and step inside. But as I start to wipe several years of dust from the seat, there's a series of rapid hammer blows to the top of my head, bam-bam-bam-bam-bam, staccato bursts of pain like a machine gun firing hot lead into my skull. Cursing energetically, I duck back through the door and make a run for the beach.

"I didn't know you were that fast," Jagular says when I arrive at the water's edge.

"Neither did I," I tell him.

Behind me, fifty yards back, a refrigerator-sized cloud of wasps buzzes a few angry circles around the outhouse, then reluctantly heads back inside.

Wasps. So small; so incredibly potent. A few drops of venom and my head throbs and pulses and the edge of my vision fades in and out of focus. Meanwhile the world throbs and pulses and radiates around me at a slightly different frequency, as if I've been knocked out of alignment with my surroundings. The immediacy of the reaction is as surprising as its intensity. From the neck up I feel like an overinflated balloon. All this from four or five stings. What would fifty be like? Or five hundred?

"Lucky again," I tell the boat.

"Not that lucky," Jagular says. "You left your toilet paper in the outhouse."

•   •   •

Later that night I pull out the chart again. Fourteen or fifteen miles of rocky shoals yet before we reach the shelter of the next islands. I pull out my handheld VHF and start flipping through channels at random, hoping for a weather forecast of some kind in plain English. Again there's a continuous marine forecast, a series of MAFOR numbers describing wind speeds, wind directions, wave heights, locations—everything I need to know. But without some kind of a code key to decipher what it all means, it's only gibberish.

I start pressing different buttons and turning dials on the radio, hoping to find something useful. Maybe I can get a local radio station, at least. But I'm not even sure if there *are* any local stations around here, or if I can receive them on a low-range VHF if they exist. I should have brought the radio's instruction manual along. Or at least figured out how to decode a marine forecast before I got here. Too late now.

"As usual," Jagular says. I ignore him.

But then I notice a button in the upper left corner of the key pad, a button that's actually labeled *Weather*. Not letting my expectations build too high, I press it. Immediately I hear a synthetic female voice speaking oddly accented English:

"...rec-re-*a*-tion-al boating forecast for the North Channel. Brought to you by Environment *Can*-ada," the robot woman says. "*Wed*nesday, July twenty-*first*," she continues, scattering stresses and syllables at random. "Northwest *winds* fifteen *knots*, increa*sing* to twenty *knots* by noon. Waves three *feet* or less."

"We have a weather forecast!" I tell the boat.

"You're an idiot," he says. After our run in through the rocks I'm not inclined to argue with him. The recording cycles through a continuous loop, so I listen once more to be sure I've got it. Seems like it must be the one we need. We're in the North Channel. Tomorrow is Wednesday—I check the watch hanging from the side deck to be sure. So. Northwest winds will put us on a broad reach. Twenty knots by noon—a bit windier than I'd like, but not impossible. Three-foot waves. Should be ok. Pretty much what we had down in Texas.

"And look how well that turned out," Jagular says.

He's right. Twenty knots is a lot of wind. We'll have to get moving early. If we're sailing by 7:00 a.m., we can reach the French Islands before noon. There's got to be some kind of beach or sheltered harbor there.

Doesn't there?

◆   ◆   ◆

A series of thunderstorms sweeps through camp all night, one after another, a series of stepping stones leading to my own little vision of hell as I try to picture the day ahead. I lie awake for hours, listening to the thunder and the rain, hearing the wind tear through the trees outside the tent. It's 4:30 a.m. A lot of wind. Very dark. Thunder. Lightning. Raindrops pelting the tent like hailstones. I roll over, pull my worn-out poncho liner over my head, and try to ignore it all.

At 6:30 a.m. the storms finally rumble to a halt overhead and I climb out of the tent to find reasonably blue skies, not too much wind. Off to the west, upwind, the skies are clear. Time to get moving.

But I don't really want to go. Even in daylight there's a rough, unsparing solitude about this stretch of the shore, as if the illusion of safety we live our lives behind has been peeled back to reveal the reality we spend most of our time avoiding. No one knows where we are. No one will be able to help us if things go wrong. The world is a bigger place from the cockpit of a small sailboat, a riskier one, perhaps, than I've let myself realize before.

I look around for an excuse to stay ashore, but the storms have stopped and there's nothing else holding us back. And I can't stay here forever anyway, no matter how inadvisable it might be to go on. Twenty knots by noon. If we're going to go at all, we have to go early.

Still hoping for some kind of miraculous reprieve, I stow the tent and pack everything as neatly as I can, lashing it all in place and tying a reef in the sail. Then I click on the weather forecast one more time. Northwest winds, twenty knots by noon, twenty-five knots by evening now. I turn off the radio before the forecast can get any worse and pull my drysuit on, tugging the zipper closed tightly. One last check: sail, leeboard, rudder, oars, everything's ready. I still can't think of any excuses.

"The hell with it, then," I tell the boat. "Let's go."

◆   ◆   ◆

Rowing out past the rocks, I start to relax. We can handle this. A mile offshore, past the rocks, I hoist the reefed sail and we're away on a broad reach. It's not bad now that we're moving. After a while I untie the reef and we continue under full sail, surging ahead at top speed, even surfing the bigger waves from time to time. Perfect sailing.

Twelve or thirteen miles farther on—three hours of sailing, maybe—we finally reach the end of the rocks. I take a deep breath and loosen my grip on the tiller, stretch my cramping fingers. Up ahead are the French Islands, a string of long narrow ridgetops that form a disjointed bony finger pointed straight at us from east to west, paralleling the shore.

"We made it," I tell Jagular, checking the chart. "The gateway to the real North Channel. From here on we'll have lots of places to duck in for shelter if we have to. That's Richelieu Island there, the fingertip. We'll land there for a bit of a break, maybe tie in a reef before going on."

It's a good decision. Turning toward the beach at the eastern end of Richelieu Island, we're suddenly hit with the full force of the wind. It's been building all morning, but with the wind behind us, sailing a broad reach or run, I never noticed. The waves are building, too, with scattered whitecaps. I drag the boat onto the rocks in the lee of the island, unzip the top of my drysuit and tie the sleeves around my waist, and set off to explore.

A large dome of bare granite rises above the beach and I scramble to the top, taking a few pictures and eating a few fresh raspberries on the way. But the morning's forecast is still echoing in my mind—twenty-five knots by evening—and before long I'm back at the boat tying in a reef. It's awfully windy now, I realize. I don't really want to go out there again.

"Faint heart ne'er won fair maid," Jagular says.

"You know," I tell him, "if we both start thinking like that, neither one of us is going to make it."

"I'll make it," he says. "It's you I'm not so sure about."

But there's no alternative unless we decide to camp here, on these boulders. And the hell with that. There's not even a flat spot for the tent. We've got to head out. With this wind we'll be able to cover a lot of miles, maybe all the way to the marina at Blind River. I wouldn't mind another night in town. I hoist the reefed sail and drag Jagular off the rocks and into the wind again. A good shove, a hop over the side, and we're off on a port tack, heading north.

By the time we're fifty yards off the beach at Richelieu Island, though, I can tell that it's much windier than it was this morning. Stupidly windy, maybe. I really need to pay more attention to that. Heading downwind the wind is all too easy to ignore—you can't feel it—but it's always there, and you're always in its power. I think about taking us right back in to shore until things die down a bit, but there's no easy way to do it. Already the waves are so big that I can't get Jagular to tack, and even if we could, I doubt we'd be able to beat back to the island anyway. And besides, according to the forecast it's going to get worse, not better. I'll have to bring us around for a gybe to get back on course, and continue on, hoping for the best.

I'm not looking forward to this gybe at all—the waves are big, the wind is strong enough to feel threatening, and it's easy to imagine the worst. But finally I take a deep breath and turn Jagular around downwind in a lull between waves, easing the boom over as we gybe onto the starboard tack. Everything goes smoothly for once, and soon we're heading east again past La Salle Island, then along the southern edge of Tonty Island and Hennepin Island. We've made it.

◆   ◆   ◆

Before long I'm wishing we hadn't. We're running before the wind and waves, the only sane heading for these conditions, paralleling the rocky shore half a mile out. One by one the rolling ranks of waves—some of them higher than my head now—are steadily overtaking us, and Jagular surfs outrageously along each crest at the very edge of control. It takes all my concentration to handle the tiller and keep us pointing straight ahead, and even so, it feels more like luck than skill. I've got the sail eased well out to port to avoid an accidental gybe. We'd never survive that. But even reefed, we're way overpowered. I think about dropping the sail to continue under oars, but I'm not even sure I could manage that without capsizing.

"The good news is, it won't be long before we reach Blind River at this speed," Jagular says as we slide off the back of yet another wave, slipping slightly to starboard as it passes beneath us.

"What's the bad news?" I ask, fighting to get us headed straight again before the next wave reaches us. There's a sudden surge as it catches us and flings us forward at the edge of control, and again it's all I can do to keep us heading straight down the face of the wave.

"For one thing, we'll have to gybe onto the port tack at Comb Point before we can head in to Blind River."

Yes, I've been worrying about that myself. Nothing I can do about it right now, though. To be honest, I'll be surprised if we make it that far.

"Is that it?" I say.

"You also forgot to put the top of your drysuit back on after landing on Richelieu Island."

Shit. He's right. The sleeves are still tied around my waist; if we go over, I won't be staying dry. Cold water will pour into the legs of my suit, dragging me down, sucking the warmth from my body. I'm a decent swimmer when I have to be, but a drysuit full of water isn't going to help. Still, there's no way I can fix that, either. Even on land, pulling on the suit is never an easy thing to do; in these conditions it'd be impossible. I can't afford to let go of the tiller for a moment. There's nothing I can do but hope for the best.

"And you see that spar buoy a half mile to starboard?" Jagular continues.

I do—a tall black marker well offshore, off the starboard bow. "What about it?" I ask.

Another wave catches us before Jagular answers. This one is so tall and steep that its crest breaks over the transom and spills into the cockpit, soaking everything and slewing the boat sideways for a moment before the rudder responds and we're back on course. A close call. It's definitely getting worse.

"So what about the buoy?" I ask again when things are back in control for the moment.

"It marks the *outer* end of the Patrick Point reef," Jagular says.

I glance over at the buoy one more time. It's more than a mile offshore, way outside our line of travel. And then another wave picks us up, lifts us higher, and I can see the line of breakers stretching across our path a half mile ahead, an unbroken wall of heaving, foaming white that reaches all the way from shore to the buoy. I should have been paying closer attention to the chart.

I start running through our options. We're on the starboard tack already—I could alter course for the buoy without worrying about a gybe. But that would put these steep waves dead on our beam. We'd never make it. And we'd be heading offshore all the while, farther and farther from safety. If we try to head for shore instead, there's a good chance we wouldn't survive the necessary gybe. Even if we did, we'd have the waves dead on our opposite beam. I could try to drop the sail altogether, but that would mean leaving the helm unattended for a few moments. And that would mean disaster.

We're screwed.

Then another wave rises up behind us, taller and steeper than the rest. The crest breaks into the cockpit while the body of the wave flings the bow violently to starboard. For an instant we're hanging sideways on the steepest part of the wave, waiting to be thrown down into the trough. This is it.

But somehow I'm already moving, pushed by a desperate need to try something before submitting to the consequences. With no thought or plan I lunge forward to the starboard side of the mast, uncleat the halyard, and let it fly. The yard drops down into the lake off our port side, dragging the reefed sail with it, and my weight is right where it needs to be, to starboard. We're beam on to the waves with a bare mast and a cockpit half filled with water.

And we're still upright.

◆   ◆   ◆

Dropping the sail has calmed things down considerably, but the waves are still rolling the half-swamped boat in a series of sickening lurches. I grab the anchor bucket and start bailing frantically, and soon manage to clear most of the water out of the cockpit. With the weight of the water gone, the boat floats lightly on the waves, safe and stable. I sit down on the rowing thwart and take a moment to look around. With the sail down we're perfectly fine out here. Remember that, I tell myself. The boat can take a lot more without the rig than it can with it. When in doubt, drop the sail. We're bobbing lightly across the water now, in no danger at all. We've gone from terror to serenity at the drop of a halyard. I pull out the chart to see if I can figure out where we've ended up.

We're drifting over the shallow bank off Patrick Point, just upwind of the reef. The chart shows a long underwater ridge at the eastern edge of the bank, where the water depth decreases suddenly—fifty feet here, three feet there. No wonder there are breaking waves.

"Speaking of which," Jagular says.

I look around. The breakers are just ahead, and we're drifting down on them rapidly in this wind. I grab the oars and start rowing for the end of the reef, but give up almost immediately. There's no way I'll be able to make enough headway in these waves to row all the way around the reef. Instead I turn us toward shore. We should be able to pull up onto a beach without needing to cross the reef.

But no. We're going to be pushed across the line of breakers—there's no way around it. I can't row fast enough to escape.

"Hang on," I tell the boat, then spin the bow toward the reef and start to row hard. There's a gap ahead, a ten-yard stretch of reef that must be deeper than the rest. The waves are smaller there, the crests barely breaking at all. With a final surge as a last wave passes, we're past the rocks and inside the breakers.

Carved into each post is an intricately detailed face.

I stop rowing and look around. We're alongside a beautiful rocky shoreline, all granite cliffs and tall pines, blue skies and sunlight, clear cool green water. I've been too busy all day to notice. I pull out the chart again. We've sailed off its edge and onto the back side, eighty miles or more since we left Michigan five days ago. Ahead lie the uncountable tangles of rocky islands and sheltered bays that make up the eastern half of the North Channel. Inadvisable or not, we've made it. Blind River and its marina are just three miles ahead, around Comb Point.

"We've done enough for today, though," I tell the boat, and start rowing toward shore instead.

Off to our left the reef runs up onto the mainland, ending in a swooping series of granite domes and slabs that rise from the water to create a natural harbor. Ahead lies a horseshoe-shaped lagoon that's completely sheltered from wind and waves, an idyllic cove of tall pines, granite cliffs, and bright sand beaches. We glide through the lagoon and nose up onto the sand, where I sponge the last of the water from the boat and climb out.

The cove is utterly deserted, an echo of the hollowness I feel after our long ordeal, our narrow escape. I have no energy left for fear, for thought, for emotion. There's only the bright sun and the glittering waves, the rustling pines and the hot sand beneath my feet. There's a terrible and impersonal beauty here, a beauty that would not have been diminished at all if we had ended up smashed to pieces on the reef this afternoon. Our presence is irrelevant, our continued existence neither asked for nor denied.

I walk down to the end of the beach, where three tall posts have been set into the ground. They're as big as tree trunks, rising ten feet above the sand. As I get closer, I start to laugh. We're not alone after all. Carved into each post is an intricately detailed face staring out at the breaking waves as if waiting to pass judgment. A grim and watchful trinity, ancient and alien and, yes, faintly disapproving. I stare at them for a long time.

"Well," I tell the first sentinel at last. "We made it, didn't we?"

Then I turn and walk slowly back down the beach, back to where Jagular is waiting at the edge of the lagoon.

Shore Leave

MORNING. I lie on the beach watching the sky as the sun floats slowly over the horizon like a brightly colored balloon. I feel no particular desire to do anything. The sun climbs higher, the sky grows bluer, and still I feel no urge to move. Whatever motivations have been driving me on have completely drained away in the wake of yesterday's close call. Finally, more out of habit than anything else, I get up and start packing.

The truth is, we could easily have capsized yesterday. Most likely that would've been nothing more than a colossal pain in the ass: wet gear, tangled lines, a lost camera, a cold swim. Even the worst I can imagine—the boat smashed on the rocks and me ashore alone—would hardly have been a life and death situation, not two miles from a major highway. The remoteness of a trip like this is largely an illusion, a willing suspension of awareness that lets small boat sailors slide along the edges of civilization without perceiving its influence.

So what I'm feeling isn't fear, exactly; it's not uncertainty, or danger. It's the unexpected shift of perception that's forced upon you when a theoretical truth suddenly manifests itself as an actual one. I always knew that any unballasted dinghy could be capsized—in theory. Now I *know*, with a jarring certainty that can't be denied or evaded.

"Apparently it takes some people longer to understand the obvious," Jagular says.

I can't argue with him. And there's a long way to go yet before the end of the trip, wherever that turns out to be. I take out my drysuit and start pulling it on. Finally we're ready—9:00 a.m., our latest start yet. I row out of the lagoon and raise the sail. Not much wind. Still, the weather forecast insists that there's a high wind warning for this evening, with northwest winds at twenty-five knots for the next few days. We have to reach the Turnbull Islands before those winds arrive—we can hole up there for as long as we need to, with plenty of shelter and places to camp—and the morning calm is not helping. I drop the sail, undo the top of my drysuit, and start rowing.

We glide along just offshore, below the tall rocky ridge whose eastern end forms Comb Point. It's a beautiful day, and I'm starting to relax a bit. As long as we can get to the Turnbulls before the wind kicks in. I start to row faster.

Luckily we don't have far to go. Once we round Comb Point I can see the marina at Blind River, with its seawall, its Canadian flag, and a dense cluster of masts that makes the harbor look like a giant pincushion from here. A mile to go. It'll be nice to get some food, call home, maybe get a shower. It's less than six miles to the Turnbulls after that.

Our good fortune continues once we reach the marina: there's a floating dock for small boats, and it's completely empty—no need to go near the big cruisers, where I'd have to endure the ritual humiliations marinas like to impose on small boat sailors: trying to climb up onto a dock meant for far bigger boats, struggling to drag gear out of the boat from a dock six feet above, Jagular bouncing around like a toy beneath me. Instead, I row up to the floating dock's low platform and arrange some docklines, shoving a couple of seat cushions over the side to serve as fenders. Then I peel off my drysuit and grab my wallet, a towel and soap, some clean clothes. Civilization does have its advantages, and as long as we're here I intend to make use of them.

A few other sailors are moving around on their big boats, looking over now and then at the floating visitor dock where we're tied off. "They're impressed," I tell Jagular. "See how they're trying to watch us without being too obvious about it? We just rowed in from the middle of nowhere, in a boat that's smaller than their dinghies, and with no engine. We've been out for almost a week, and come all the way from Michigan, while they've been sitting around in the marina. They're probably a little intimidated."

"Maybe," Jagular says. "Or they could just be wondering how you're going to get ashore."

I look around. The floating dock is moored in the middle of the harbor, attached to dry land only by a pair of long swooping chains that hang so low they're four feet beneath the water at the midpoint.

◆   ◆   ◆

After a BLT from the marina café and a payphone call to my brother to let him know we're still afloat, I wade back out through chest-deep water to the visitor dock. It's already after noon, and the skies are gray and cloudy. I spend a few minutes refining my reefing system, then climb back into my drysuit, drop the sail, and row out past the seawall as the onlookers on their big boats watch from the safety of their slips. We're still the only boat moving, but we've got a nice northwest breeze for now, which puts us on a broad reach toward the Turnbull Islands. Before long I take out the reef and we keep moving on, completely in control.

In a little more than an hour we're threading our way between islands, looking for a campsite that's sheltered from the northwest. I want someplace we can stay for a while. We sail past Gibson Island and its tiny satellite, O'Dwyer—nothing there. A couple of big sloops go by, heading east, one motoring and one sailing. (Sailing! It's the first sail we've seen here in the North Channel besides our own). Everyone's looking for shelter from the approaching high winds.

We keep going south past Sanford Island, the biggest in the group. Still nothing. We stop briefly on the rocky slabs of Caroline Island, where I find an eyeless gull carcass left on a boulder like a pagan sacrifice, a distant echo of Africa Rock. It's a beautiful island, but the cove we've landed in is open to the northwest, just wrong for the weather that's coming. And besides, for no reason at all I'm suddenly sure that there are bears on Caroline Island, sure that the gull sacrifice is a ruse to lure unsuspecting sailors ashore where they can be harassed and eaten. The feeling is so definite that I expect a bear to come whoofing out of the woods at any moment to ransack my gear and drag away all my food. So we leave Caroline Island and continue eastward, along the southern edge of a sudden tight cluster of islands. The wind drops to almost nothing while the clouds balloon into huge and threatening shapes overhead, and we ghost along, expecting another smiting at any moment. There's got to be a nice sheltered beach somewhere.

And there is—but there's a kayak and a tent there already. It could be the only good camping beach in the Turnbulls. I'm tempted to pull in and set up my tent at the opposite end of the beach, but I'm in no mood for company. He probably isn't, either. Or, worse—maybe he is. I turn east instead, heading farther into the maze of islands. The islands are rocky and thick with pines and brush, which won't make it easy to find a place to set up the tent. But just a couple of islands past the kayaker, we find a U-shaped beach, a tiny harbor protected by rocky wings. A perfect campsite, much better than the one we just passed. I can't help grinning.

"You're not going back to your theories about relative happiness, are you?" Jagular asks.

"Nope," I tell him as we glide up onto shore. "I'm absolutely happy this time."

I climb out and look around. We're surrounded by a scattering of rocky islands and narrow channels, a dark silent forest splintered into pieces and spread out across the water all around us like a jigsaw puzzle ready for assembly. A narrow crescent of flat, sandy beach, a perfectly sheltered bay. A beautiful sunset. An eagle soaring overhead. Whistling happily, I pull out the tent and start looking for the best spot.

Later that evening I take Jagular out for a row—the high winds promised by the forecast still haven't arrived. Or if they have, they're not touching us here. It's good to be rowing just because I want to, with no need to cover a lot of miles, the empty boat floating lightly for a change. We glide along, smooth and silent, the oars dipping soundlessly into the water at each stroke.

At the edge of the islands a big sloop motors past, looking for somewhere to anchor for the night. They're close enough that I can hear the voices of people on board over the drone of the outboard. "That's the guy with the little sailboat," I hear someone say. "He was at the marina this morning. He stayed about an hour, then left."

"See?" I tell Jagular. "They remember us. I told you people were impressed."

"*Memorable* and *impressive* are not synonyms," Jagular says.

◆   ◆   ◆

The next day begins with a hushed calm and overcast skies. I decide to take advantage of the lack of wind and row the mile-long crossing to Round Island, which rises above the water like a lonely fortress guarding the northeastern entrance to the Turnbulls. I leave Jagular on a rocky beach at the foot of a towering wall of granite and spend the day climbing Round Island's steep cliffs and wading through the ankle-deep mosses and lichens that lie scattered around the forest floor like giant green brains, trying to avoid the huge spiders that hang from every tree. That evening we head back to the Turnbulls, where I take an alternate route back to our campsite, cutting through a sheltered bay just west of Turnbull Island.

The bay must be the main anchorage for the area. More than a dozen deep-keeled cruising boats are here to wait out the weather. It's too late to avoid being seen, so I keep rowing. But they're a friendly bunch, it turns out—each boat crew calls me over as I row past, wanting to know where I've come from, where I'm going. Everyone seems to think I'm crazy to have come this far in a boat this small. At the same time, they're secretly envious.

"You're delusional," Jagular says.

Maybe. But here they are, all stuck at anchor while we're off exploring. Now that they've arrived, they have nowhere to go and nothing to do. They're all sitting around talking and drinking beer, cooking hamburgers on portable grills hanging from the lifelines, or motoring around aimlessly in ugly inflatable dinghies. No one seems to know what else to do. Sailing was supposed to bring a brief respite from their harried, over-cluttered lives, but their boats are too big and too fancy—they've brought all the clutter with them. Now they're wondering why they bothered. Bug zappers hang from the rigging overhead, casting faint blue shadows over everything. Radios play softly. The rattle of onboard generators echoes around the bay. It's a floating campground filled with fat sloops instead of double-axle trailers. Cockpits instead of campfires.

That's probably why people aboard big boats are so keen to give things away—they're embarrassed by how little we small boat sailors seem to need. No engine. No electronics. No appliances. No cabin, even. Our presence here is a silent reproach, a reminder of how badly they've botched it. As a result, there's a hurried consignment of goods at each stop, an attempt to offload some of the embarrassment and, at the same time, make us complicit in their failure to escape the oppressive conveniences of life ashore. Cans of ice-cold Coca-Cola straight from an onboard refrigerator. Fancy cheeses and crackers. British novels where, in elegantly restrained prose, nothing ever happens. Hamburgers hot from the grill. Orange juice. Ice cream. Each gift is an attempt at expiation. An act of penance.

"Or maybe they just like sharing," Jagular says. "Maybe they feel sorry for you."

"Well, they should feel sorry for themselves—we're fine. Our way of sailing may be less comfortable than theirs, but it's a hell of a lot more rewarding. I refuse to become a victim of their seductive ideology."

"Someone gives you a burger and a Coke and it's an ideology? You're incredible," Jagular says.

"Thank you."

"Incredible in the sense of impossible to believe."

"It doesn't matter whether you want to believe it or not," I say. "We live in a system designed to create artificial needs by selling the idea that comfort and happiness are the same thing. The idea is absurd, but it's been repeated so often that no one thinks to question it anymore."

"No one except you," Jagular says.

"Well, there aren't many of us."

I stop rowing and let the boat glide through the water for a moment, looking back at the crowded anchorage. Someone on the foredeck of a big fiberglass sloop gives me a friendly wave. With a sigh, I snap open a Coke before waving back. Might as well enjoy it before it gets warm.

◆   ◆   ◆

Back at camp I start thinking about our next step. If it's still not too windy by morning, we can probably make the next hop over to the Whalesback Channel before it gets bad. I decide to be ready just in case. I rinse all my clothes out and hang them up to dry, refill my water bottles, clean the stove, all the small chores I never bother with while we're moving. When I pull out my drysuit to turn it inside-out for a good airing, though, I find a small hole in the foot. The suit cost me more than the entire boat, and now it's useless. I dig through my repair kit, wondering what I can do about it. Pocket knife. Screwdriver. Spare tiller bolt. Crescent wrench. Vise-grip pliers. Spare line. Small tub of epoxy. A couple of fiberglass patches. A roll of duct tape. Why not, I decide, and put a multi-layered patch over the hole, inside and out. Better than nothing.

The next day I'm up at dawn to load the gear for an early start. If it's too bad we can always turn back. I pull on my duct-taped drysuit and row out through the maze of channels, stopping at a small gravel beach in the lee of an unnamed island at the northern edge of the Turnbulls. From here I can see our proposed route, five miles of open water to the western edge of the Whalesback Channel. Once we're there it'll be easy sailing, with lots of places to pull in if things start to get rough. It's pretty windy already, though, with a flurry of whitecaps surging eastward across the water as if in a hurry to get there ahead of us. If we're going to miss the worst of it, we'll have to go soon.

"Well," I say after a moment, "at least we'll be headed downwind."

"Just like we were when you almost capsized us the last time," Jagular says.

I step the mast and start tying a reef in the sail anyway, adjusting the halyard and downhaul. After checking the zipper on my drysuit one more time, I pull the boat into knee-deep water, hoist the sail, and hop in. We're off, sailing eastward toward the Whalesback Channel.

"Or to a watery grave, whichever comes first," the boat suggests. I ignore him.

◆   ◆   ◆

It's windy enough, but not too bad with a reef in. I moved the halyard closer to the center of the yard before I hoisted the sail this time, so there's almost an equal amount of sail on each side of the mast now. We're nicely balanced on our downwind heading now. I should have thought of this sooner. We're moving fast but perfectly in control.

"For now," Jagular says, but I ignore him again. I'm too busy trying to read the chart and figure out where we should go, which is never easy in a small boat. One hand for the tiller, one for the mainsheet; one hand for the chart, one for the compass. Eventually, by tucking the tiller under my arm and cleating off the sheet with a slippery hitch that will, in theory, allow me to tug it free in a gust in time to prevent a capsize, I get a good enough look at things to make a decision. We'll hug the northern side of the Whalesback Channel and cut into Beardrop Harbour, a narrow east-west anchorage sheltered by a rocky ridge of islands paralleling the shore like a castle wall. There's another small island in the center of the harbor that will offer perfect shelter once we get there.

Halfway across to Beardrop Harbour the wind drops off in a sudden lull. I've become skeptical of sudden calms, though, and decide to wait a while before taking the reef out. I lean back against the side deck. The sail hangs limp above the cockpit. The sky grows darker. Soon the promised winds arrive, dragging a dark line of gusty shadows across the surface of the water behind us. We're about to be moving fast. Very fast.

"Hey, I did the smart thing there," I tell the boat as I take a last look around to make sure we're ready. "We'd really be in trouble if I had taken out that reef."

"Even a blind pig roots up an acorn every now and then," Jagular says.

Then the wind is on us and we're off on a screaming run toward Beardrop Harbour and the Whalesback Channel. Three miles to go. We'll probably make it.

◆   ◆   ◆

It's windy, all right; maybe windier than it was off Patrick Point. We shoot past Godfrey Island. LaFrance Rock. Chapman Rock. I'm too busy with the sheet and tiller to risk another look at the chart, but we've got to be close to the entrance to Beardrop Harbour. I'm watching the northern shore closely for an opening. And there it is, a long narrow channel that runs due east between tall cliffs on the northern shore of the Whalesback Channel—a dead run in on a port tack. Way more wind than I want, but we should be able to tuck in behind the small island in the middle of the harbor and find some shelter. It's a perfect set-up, actually, except for one thing: to make the turn to starboard behind the island, we'll need to gybe.

"Do you notice how this is starting to look familiar?" Jagular says, as a new gust hits and sends us surfing down the face of a wave.

We're still mostly in control, though, and before long we're past the outer channel and nearing the island that protects the inner anchorage. We just have to cut in behind it and we'll be safely out of the wind.

"Hang on," I tell the boat. "We're tacking." I push the tiller over and turn us into the wind. We'll come about to reach our new heading instead of gybing. Slower, but safer.

"In theory, anyway," Jagular says, and shudders to a stop, bow into the wind, then falls off, still on the port tack. I bring us off the wind to regain some speed, then try again. But the waves are too big for us to punch through. And our two failed tacks have used up all the room available in the narrow channel. We're about to be aground on the rocky shore of Beardrop Harbour. It's awfully windy. Awfully rocky. This will be ugly.

"Hell with it, then," I say, and swing the tiller the other way instead. We might as well crash into the water instead of onto the rocks. We fall off the wind once more, and this time I keep turning. The bow surges past the rocks just inches away, and I reach up to grab the boom as the sail gybes across to the starboard tack. Somehow I've handled it perfectly. Scooting along on a beam reach, Jagular sails into the lee of the high rocky island in the middle of Beardrop Harbour and glides to a gentle stop in its wind shadow.

◆   ◆   ◆

Almost before I get the tent set up, tucked under a tall pine in the center of Beardrop Harbour's tiny island, we're approached by an outboard-powered inflatable dinghy overflowing with a small blonde boy and two large dogs. The dinghy is riding so low in the water, and the dogs are wriggling and jumping so excitedly, that I'll be surprised if they make it to our island without swamping. The boy at the tiller is grinning widely, oblivious to it all.

"See that?" I tell Jagular. "I love to see a kid out on his own without any adults hovering over him. All the kids his age back home are probably busy riding their bikes down sidewalks, wearing helmets and kneepads while their parents run alongside, horrified at the thought of a scraped knee, which would immediately get doused in anti-bacterial antibiotic ointments and wrapped in sterile gauze. Everything these days is expected to be safe and supervised, with no one allowed to make the kind of stupid mistakes you need to make to learn. As a result, everyone grows up terrified and incompetent, ready to hand over all their decisions to "experts" who don't know any better than they do anyway."

"Why doesn't it surprise me that you would be in favor of making stupid mistakes?" Jagular says.

At that moment one of the dogs, a big brown Labrador, lurches into the water while the dinghy is still ten yards offshore. Straining to hold his head above the surface, the Lab thrashes his way desperately to shore, where he crawls onto the rocks at my feet and does a full-body shake that throws him so far off balance he topples back into the water and starts thrashing around again in the shallows. At the same time, the dinghy drives at full speed up onto the rocks, the outboard bouncing a couple of times off the rocky bottom, and the other dog—an elegant white Samoyed with pale blue eyes—steps daintily onto the island.

"Hi!" says the young boy loudly, stumbling out of the dinghy and throwing the painter onto the rocks without tying it to anything. "I'm Caleb!" Meanwhile the Lab has scrabbled clumsily out of the water again and is busy gobbling down a dead fish he's found at the water's edge. The Samoyed looks on disdainfully. With a particularly enthusiastic lurch the Lab throws the decaying fish into the air and stumbles headlong into the water again. Left to its own devices, the outboard motor sputters to a reluctant halt. The Lab keeps thrashing desperately in the water, barely able to hold his head up high enough to breathe, but Caleb pays him no attention.

"That's an awfully small tent—is that yours? I get to sleep in the double bed aboard my grandpa's boat and that's a lot bigger than your tent. You should get a bigger tent. And a bigger boat. What's your name?" he asks suddenly, then goes on without waiting for an answer. "My grandpa and I are sailing. We go every summer. We came in this afternoon on that boat." He points back at a sloop anchored out in the harbor. Then without warning he swings his arm around to point toward the high cliffbound island at the southeast end of Beardrop Harbour, almost clobbering me in the ear. "Want to go on an expedition over there? My grandpa doesn't want me going by myself but he said if you came it would be ok."

Before I can answer, the Lab finally crawls out of the water again and collapses beside us, dropping the rotting fish carcass on my bare feet. An elderly gentleman aboard the sloop—the grandpa, I assume—climbs out of the cabin, looks around for a moment, and sees us standing together on the island. He gives me a wave and gleefully disappears below decks.

"That's my grandpa. He doesn't ever come ashore," says the boy, and crawls back into his dinghy. The Samoyed steps daintily aboard behind him. The Lab groans loudly and drags himself to his feet, gobbles down the entire dead fish in a series of great hacking gulps, and then thrashes into the water and scrabbles uselessly at the side of the dinghy with his front paws until the boy drags him aboard by the collar.

"We have to go now so I can be back in time for supper, though," the boy says. He yanks the cord on the outboard three or four times until it starts with a smoky sputter and drags the entire ensemble—dinghy, boy, Lab, and Samoyed—backwards off the rocks and into deep water. "Come on!" the boy calls, and shifts the motor into forward gear with a shuddering clunk. The overloaded dinghy starts creeping toward the cliffs at the far side of the island. The Lab hangs his head over the side and vomits up the fish head, retching so violently that he falls overboard and has to be dragged back into the boat by the collar again while the dinghy circles aimlessly around the rocks, bouncing off the island now and then. Finally the boy gets the dog aboard and grabs the tiller again.

"Let's go," he says, and sputters off in a cloud of blue smoke.

"What I like most about these trips is the solitude," Jagular says. "The unspoiled and pristine silence of the great northern wilderness."

I shake my head sadly. "Me, too."

The old man aboard the sloop pops his head out of the cabin and gives me another cheery wave, disappearing again before I can protest. With a sigh I drag the boat into the water and start rowing after the overloaded inflatable. I can hear the Lab choking and snuffling on fishbones all the way across the harbor.

◆   ◆   ◆

We find a break in the cliffs about a mile away, where I'm able to drag Jagular up onto a rock. Despite Caleb's head start, we've beaten him here; the outboard motor quit two or three times on the trip through the harbor. When the overloaded dinghy finally arrives, the Samoyed steps gently onto the rock and looks up at me calmly. The Lab lurches into the water and splashes his way up beside us, then turns to look back at Caleb.

"Hey, I forgot my shoes!" Caleb says as the bow of the dinghy bounces off the rock. "I'll be right back!" He shifts the outboard into reverse with another unhealthy clunk, leaving me standing on the rock beside the two dogs. The Samoyed looks up at me once more, then settles calmly at my feet. The Lab paces nervously back and forth, whining softly.

"It's ok," I tell the Lab. "He'll be right back."

I hope.

But the Lab keeps pacing back and forth across the small boulder, watching the boy and the dinghy get farther and farther away. Even the Samoyed is getting nervous; she stands up and presses herself against my leg, staring out at the sputtering dinghy half a mile across the harbor. It's too much for the Lab; he throws his body into the water and starts thrashing after the boy. He sinks lower and lower with each stroke, until only his eyes and the tip of his nose are above water. The boy never looks back—he's halfway to the sloop by now. The Lab is thrashing around thirty yards offshore. He'll never make it.

"I thought Labrador Retrievers were good swimmers," I tell the boat.

"Not all of them, apparently," Jagular says.

I'm about to jump into the boat and start rowing to the rescue when the Lab seems to realize he's not going to make it. Still mostly submerged, he paddles in a desperate circle back to the rock and crawls out at my feet, whining weakly.

"Good boy," I tell him, and pat his head comfortingly. "That's a good dog."

"Good for what, is what I'd like to know," Jagular says.

◆   ◆   ◆

Twenty long minutes later the boy is back with his shoes. The Lab is overjoyed, jumping and bounding all over the rock, somehow managing not to fall in. The Samoyed wags her tail. Caleb steps onto the rock and immediately starts climbing higher onto the cliffs, the dinghy's painter tossed carelessly onto the rock behind him—again, not tied to anything. The dogs follow him, jostling around his feet.

"Hey!" Caleb shouts, already halfway up the cliffs. "Blueberries, lots of them! Come on!"

"Don't look at me," Jagular says. "You're the chaperone. I'm just the boat."

"Thanks," I tell him. With a sigh, I start climbing.

It's not too bad, though. We quickly reach the top of the cliffs and spend a half hour wandering around enjoying the views over the Whalesback Channel, taking pictures, and eating fresh blueberries—they're everywhere. Then it's back down to the boats for the trip back across Beardrop Harbour. The Samoyed steps calmly into the inflatable and sits down at the bow. Caleb coaxes the terrified Lab in after her, and then pulls the starter cord on the outboard. Nothing. He tries again—still nothing.

"Let me give you a hand," I tell him. I pull the dinghy around so I can reach the cord from the rock, and I give it a good yank. Nothing. I pull harder. The entire cord unwraps itself from the flywheel and comes off in my hand.

"And I thought you were bad at *sailing*," Jagular says.

"My grandpa just fixed the motor yesterday!" Caleb says. "He's not going to be happy."

◆   ◆   ◆

By the time we get rid of Caleb and his dogs, it's early evening. Beardrop Harbour is full. There must be twenty boats tucked in behind our island. When we arrived, there were three or four. With so many big, heavily ballasted boats seeking shelter in this wind, I'm glad we're safely ashore. Even here in the protection of our sheltered cove it was a long pull into the wind to get back to our campsite.

I'm just starting to pull out my stove to make supper when another boat comes sailing in: a low, sleek wooden sharpie about thirty feet long, sailing under jib alone—it really *is* windy. There's a dark-haired woman on the fore-deck, and a black-bearded man at the tiller. The boat surges joyfully through the waves, and the whole scene exudes a soulful jauntiness that's been entirely missing from the other sailboats I've seen. A wooden boat—and they're actually under sail, with no outboard in sight! I scramble to the top of my rocky island and snap some photos as they shoot into the harbor and round up behind the island to anchor a quarter mile out.

After a hasty supper of Ramen noodles and cheese sauce, I decide to row over and visit them. They've tied up next to another sloop, a big white high-sided plastic trough of a boat about thirty-five feet long. I'm amazed at the difference between them: the elegant sharpie sits low in the water, barely higher than Jagular, while the slab-sided plastic boat towers so high above that the tip of Jagular's mast barely reaches the cockpit. I row toward them, and when I'm near enough to ship the oars and coast in, call out in warning: "Anybody home?"

"Here we go," Jagular says. "Back to mooching off of the big boats."

"Nonsense," I tell him as we glide closer. "I'm bringing gifts this time, not taking them. I know how hard it is to get pictures of your own boat under sail, so I'm going to offer them some photos."

There are four of them: Hugh and Julie on the sharpie, Dave and Ann in the other boat. Everyone greets us cheerfully, and we're quickly invited to tie up alongside. They all have lots of questions: where have we come from, where are we headed, how long have we been out? They're the first people I've met who seem genuinely interested in the idea of cruising in a homebuilt sailboat the size of a kayak. And they take my implied claim to be a sailor seriously, I can see, accepting me among them as if I actually belong there. I'm a bit nervous, knowing that my acceptance is mostly undeserved. Still, here we are, and everyone seems happy to have me join them.

Hugh—a professional sailor and tall ship captain in real life, it turns out—is happy to accept my offer to send him copies of my photos. He built the sharpie himself, as I suspected, and has never managed to get good pictures of it sailing. Dave, the captain of the ugly plastic boat—a former junior high math teacher who's so soft spoken and laid back he seems more like a surfer in exile—is interested, too.

"Did you get any shots of my boat?" he asks.

"No," I say. "I'm sorry I missed you. When did you come in?"

"I was right behind them," he says.

There's a brief silence. I look at the sharpie, then at the ugly plastic boat, and shrug. Dave shakes his head sadly, and nobody says anything. Julie finally steps in to invite me aboard for supper—fresh venison steaks, baked potatoes, red wine. Everyone agrees that I should stay a while.

"See?" Jagular says as I climb into the sharpie's cockpit. "Mooching again."

"You be quiet," I whisper. "These people are professional sailors—they won't put up with you sassing them."

"What's that?" Dave asks.

"Nothing," I tell him. "Never mind."

◆   ◆   ◆

I enjoy a few hours with my new friends, who seem to have done a lot more sailing than I have but are too nice to admit it—or rather, too nice to care. I row away feeling like I've found some people I belonged with for a change, and wondering if I'll ever run into them again.

"See?" I tell Jagular as I drag him ashore on our island for the night. "I'm not as much of a misanthropist as you suppose. I liked them, didn't I?"

"Four out of seven billion," the boat says. "I rest my case."

I'm too tired, and too happy, to bother answering him.

The next morning I'm up early again. Last night's winds have been replaced with a bright cloudless morning. A low golden slanting light shines across the harbor, and the water is a smooth, dark reflection of the surrounding pines. Out in the harbor the big boats all float around aimlessly, anchor lines drooping. I quietly pack up the tent and gear, waiting for someone else to wake up. But no one does. Finally I slide Jagular into the water and shove off from shore. We drift around for a few minutes between the big boats. Still nothing.

"Big boat people are late sleepers," I tell the boat.

"It's not even seven a.m."

"Still."

But the big boats all just float there silently, and the sun still slants its golden light over the harbor, and the air is cool and still, and everything is packed, and there's nothing left to do. Finally I start rowing, letting the oars float themselves silently into the water on each stroke, pulling so gently there's barely a ripple. We slide through the anchorage alone, slipping quietly out through a narrow channel bordered by tall cliffs. A family of minks swims across the channel just ahead of us, their wake etching a long V across the smooth water.

Soon we're out into the Whalesback Channel again, threading our way between a series of rocky islands that rise in parallel ridges from the water. A faint northerly breeze sets in, just enough wind to keep us moving faster than rowing speed, so I hoist the sail. Satisfied, I set the self-steering lines and let the boat mind itself. We sail eastward up the channel toward wherever we're going next. At the moment I'm too lazy to pull out the chart and choose a destination.

◆   ◆   ◆

At the eastern edge of the Whalesback Channel, past the great granite domes of Greenway Island and Norquay Island, the wind picks up. Still not sure where we're going, I decide to head as far north as we can—we can always turn downwind later if we need to, but any miles to windward we lose

We slide through the anchorage alone.

now will be hard to make up. It's a cold beat, sailing close-hauled on a port tack, and I pause to pull on my drysuit. Much nicer. We're taking lots of spray aboard, but now that I'm warm and dry it doesn't matter. I line up a spot on the southern tip of Papineau Island to aim for, three and half miles away to the northeast. In this wind we might just be able to reach it in one tack.

My guess is right on—we touch down on Papineau Island just where I thought we would. Either I made a lucky guess or I'm getting better at recognizing just how far to windward Jagular can sail.

"Lucky guess," Jagular says.

"Well, sometimes it's better to be lucky than good," I tell him. "Besides, who cares? Take a look—we just sailed across the Whalesback Channel, and it's a beautiful day, and all those big boats are probably still anchored back in Beardrop Harbour missing all the fun."

"Isn't that Hugh and Julie's boat there?" Jagular asks. "And Dave and Ann?"

He's right. Hugh's long lean sharpie is slicing through the waves well to the south of us, out in the middle of the Whalesback Channel, heading east toward the Ontario mainland. My map shows a town in that direction with the unlikely name—considering the region's French heritage—of Spanish. That seems to be where they're headed. Dave's sloop is alongside Hugh's sharpie, but pulling slightly ahead. The gap grows slowly wider as we watch.

"What do you know?" I tell Jagular. "Dave must be a good sailor to be beating Hugh. Then again, he is a retired math teacher. I guess all that 'The shortest distance between two points is a straight line' stuff really works."

I pull out my camera and zoom in on the boats, snap some photos—I'm careful to get lots of pictures of Dave's boat this time. It may be ugly, but they're actually sailing, unlike almost every other big boat I've seen on the North Channel. I'm not even sure Hugh's boat has an engine—and although I know Dave's boat has one, he hasn't used it at all.

"How a boat looks isn't that important anyway," I tell Jagular. "What matters is how it sails. That's why I never used to mind when people would ask my brother 'Is that an antique?' or 'Did you build it yourself?' when they saw his boat, and then hurry past you without saying anything."

"But his boats always sail better than we do, too," Jagular points out. I pretend not to hear him, and take a few final photographs before packing my camera away. Then, indecision gone, I pull Jagular into the water again and head off to the east, toward Spanish. With luck, I'll run into my new friends at the marina there.

"Do you even know if Spanish has a marina?" Jagular asks.

I don't bother to answer him. We'll find out soon enough.

◆   ◆   ◆

By the time we hit Spanish, the wind has shifted to a westerly. It's been getting steadily stronger since we left Papineau Island, too. We probably should be reefed. Instead we're flying along on a dead run, the sail eased way out and the boat surfing along, moving fast. Up ahead I can see what looks like a lighthouse, and a set of rocky seawalls, and a bristling of masts within the harbor.

"See?" I tell Jagular. "There's a marina."

We come in through a break in the seawall on a screaming run, heading due east through the harbor, past row after row of boats waiting alone in their slips. Up ahead, the fuel dock and boat ramp stand at the eastern end of the marina. I sail toward them, then push the tiller over when we're ten feet out. Jagular slides onto a beam reach heading north along the fuel dock, the tip of the boom just a few feet away from the pilings. As we reach the end of the fuel dock I turn us into the wind past the boat ramp and come alongside the visitor's dock at the north side of the harbor. We glide to a stop, parked neatly alongside the dock without so much as a bump, and pointed dead into the wind, sail flapping gently—a perfect landing. Julie is standing on the dock waiting to take our bow line, which—incredibly—I've had the foresight to prepare ahead of time. I reach over and hand the line to her as we coast to a stop.

"Great," Jagular says. "Now they really *will* think you're a decent sailor."

But there's nothing he can do about it. It really was a perfect landing. Even better, a *flashy* landing, a series of maneuvers executed with the daring nonchalance and swashbuckling panache that I always aspire to—secretly—but am rarely able to pull off. And this time there are witnesses. I can't help grinning as Julie helps me tie up the boat, and then we're all together again: Hugh and Julie, Dave and Ann, and me. They're heading into town to buy groceries. I grab my wallet and join them.

The Devil's Horn

WE LEAVE SPANISH EARLY THE NEXT MORNING, headed east for Little Detroit, the narrow passage that serves as the eastern entrance to the Whalesback Channel. The time ashore has been a pleasant reprieve: a shower, a few groceries, the chance to do laundry, and a few more hours hanging out with my friends. Hugh even invites us to stop by his house later in our cruise. The vague directions he offers—somewhere on the south side of some island I'll be passing at some point—make that unlikely, but I appreciate the gesture.

But now they're gone and it's just Jagular and me again. We're headed for the Benjamin Islands, a fabled archipelago of pink granite and tall pines, a world of hidden coves and secret anchorages and steep-sided bays lined with sandy beaches. From what I've heard about the North Channel, the Benjamins are so beautiful, and so popular, that I'm a little afraid we'll find them over-run with powerboaters. Still, I have to see them for myself. Maybe we'll get lucky and there won't be anyone there. Besides, the Benjamins have been my secret destination all along. Once we get there I'll feel ready to turn back. If we head west along the north side of Manitoulin Island after stopping off in the Benjamin Islands, we can make a giant loop of our trip, and sail back into the harbor at De Tour Village without needing to retrace our steps.

"Sailing west," Jagular says. "Against the prevailing winds."

Given our usual windward performance, I'm as skeptical as he is. Getting back to De Tour Village won't be fast. It might not even be possible. I've got a back-up plan, though: if I have to, I can leave Jagular here in Spanish, catch a bus to Michigan, and drive back with the car and trailer to pick him up. But I'm hoping I won't have to do that. Sailing back would be a much more satisfying end to our travels. Carving a sweeping circle around the edges of the North Channel, imposing the cyclic structure and coherence of a classic *Bildungsroman* on our adventures.

"Except in a *Bildungsroman* the hero actually learns something from his self-imposed exile," Jagular says. "He matures. He evolves. He learns to accept his place within the community, and returns home to become a productive member of society."

"So?"

"You haven't learned anything," the boat says. "You're the same as you ever were."

"Maybe I've learned that I don't need to make any changes, then," I tell him. "Maybe I've been doing it right all along."

"No, more likely you're just not the hero," Jagular suggests. "You've probably been assigned a bit part. The guy who sells Romeo the poison, that's you. Important enough in his way, but—"

"The *apothecary?*" I protest. "I've got to be important enough for Mercutio, at least. I know most of the lines already." I start staggering around, gasping and dying, smiling bravely even as I describe the mortal wound I've just received: "*No, 'tis not so deep as a well, nor wide as a church door, but 'tis enough; 'twill serve. Ask for me tomorrow and you shall find me a grave man.*"

"That may be about right," the boat says. "If tomorrow is anything like the last few days have been, anyway."

•   •   •

On the chart, the Benjamin Islands form the western half of a swooping swirl of rock, with Fox Island to the northeast forming the rest, and a scattering of pink rocks known as the Sow and Pigs filling in the gaps to the south. It's as if a huge meteor struck here long ago, sending a pool of super-heated magma into a slow clockwise spin until the gradual settling and cooling of geology slowed the swirling mass into its present form. I've read about magnetic anomalies around the Benjamins, quirks and flaws that make compasses un-reliable, so maybe my meteor theory isn't as fanciful as it sounds. Maybe there's a huge chunk of interstellar iron bur-ied in the lake bed.

We head out early from Spanish in a light morning breeze. Not much wind. Soon I'm rowing, our usual light air tactics already in play. I rub some more wax on the oarlocks to stop their infernal squeaking, though, and after that it's pleasant enough. Before long a nice westerly kicks in and we're able to sail through the narrow, cliffbound channel of Little Detroit. It's a perfect spot for an ambush—back in the seventeenth century an Ojibwe band defeated a force of invading Iroquois warriors here by sending their women into the narrow gap as bait while they rained arrows on the Iroquois from the clifftops—but all I have to do is dodge a couple of big sailboats motoring through from east to west. Their sails are furled, of course, with sail covers lashed down tight and tidy; they won't be needed anytime soon.

"Doesn't anybody sail around here besides Hugh and Dave?" I ask the boat when we're through.

"You really expected them to short-tack through the channel, dead into the wind?"

"Well, no—but it annoys me to see brute technology serving as a replacement for skill and experience. In the old days they would have been more patient about it. They would have anchored on the eastern side to wait for a favorable wind instead of barging right on through, relying on their engines."

"In the really old days," Jagular says, "they would have enslaved a bunch of locals and forced them to row through the gap. Maybe we should go back to *those* old days."

"We don't have to go *back* to those old days—we're still there," I tell the boat. "It's just that today's evildoers do a better job of hiding their raping and plundering. Hedge funds, junk bonds, derivatives, mortgage-backed securities—Walmart—whatever they're calling it these days. The little guy does all the work, and the fat cats sit back and grab the loot. We're all galley slaves."

"Calling bankers and CEOs 'evildoers' is a bit of a stretch," Jagular says.

"Nonsense—the love of money is the root of all evil," I announce grandly. "You know how everyone goes around with those stupid *'What Would Jesus Do?'* bracelets and bumper stickers these days? Well, I can tell you what he'd do. He'd throw the goddamn money changers out of the temple, that's what he'd do. He knew that wealth and virtue are inherently incompatible—fat man, eye of the needle, blessed are the poor, all that."

"You're ranting now," Jagular says calmly. "Misquoting, too: it's a camel, not a fat man, and it's 'poor in spirit,' not just 'poor.'"

"Maybe. But I can tell you, it's a lot easier to be poor in spirit when you're poor for real, too. Wealth is a dangerous thing. In fact, now that I think of it, we probably have a Christian duty to protect people from its seductive temptations. I should be robbing banks."

"You'd get caught right away if you tried. Besides, you're not much of a Christian anyway."

"I was just *quoting* Christ!" I say.

"For your own purposes," the boat replies. "Even the Devil can quote Scripture."

"Now I'm the Devil?"

"If the shoe fits," Jagular says, and I can't think of anything to say to that. We drift around for a few moments in silence. Slowly, though, I feel myself starting to smile.

The Devil! That doesn't sound so bad after all—it just depends whose side of the story you listen to. Satan is, after all, the one truly heroic figure of Milton's *Paradise Lost*, where he serves as an archetype of individualism and defiance, a mythic symbol of man's refusal to submit blindly to the cruel and arbitrary forces that rule the universe. A pre-Byronic anti-hero sneering at convention, forging his own path through life without regard for precedent or boundary. Master of his own fate, captain of his soul. Of course, Milton couldn't openly claim that Satan was the hero when he published his poem or he would have been burned as a heretic, but anyone who has read *Paradise Lost* knows the truth.

"You *haven't* read it, though," Jagular says.

"I tried, but it was all in Italian or something."

"You're thinking of Dante," Jagular says. "Milton wrote in English."

"Whatever. All right, so I haven't read *Paradise Lost*. But I've read what everyone else has to say about it. That's practically the same thing."

There's a pained silence before Jagular answers. "The sad thing is, you have no trouble passing yourself off as an educated man."

I ignore him, still thinking about the possibilities. No, I decide. Playing the part of the Devil doesn't sound too bad at all.

"*Please allow me to introduce myself,*" I sing. "*I'm a ma-an… of wealth and taste.*"

"All right," the boat says. "You win. You're not the Devil. "

◆   ◆   ◆

Once we're through Little Detroit the wind starts to pick up. Somewhere farther along on this heading are the Hiesordt Rocks, which I need to avoid, but the waves are building so quickly that I'm having trouble spotting them. We're thumping along through the whitecaps and I really should be thinking about reefing. The wind is more like a sustained gust than a wind now. The mast creaks and strains in its step, and the rudder hums so violently I can feel the vibrations through the tiller like a faint buzz of electricity. The sail stretches tight until I can almost hear the grommets popping. Something is going to break. We're on a run again, too, starting to surf down the waves and slew sideways in the troughs, ready to broach and capsize.

And for what? I ask myself. We're not on any schedule.

"It doesn't matter!" I shout joyfully. "We don't have to keep going!" I swing the bow into the wind—again, the full force of the breeze is staggering now that we're not running downwind anymore—and drop the sail neatly into the cockpit. There are a couple of islands off to the south, and they look perfectly pleasant and inviting. I pull out the oars and start rowing toward them, whistling happily.

"I'm impressed," the boat says. "You actually seem to have learned something after all."

"I'm not as dumb as I look, remember," I tell him, still rowing.

"Not always, anyway."

It's hard to tell from this far out, but it looks like there might be a bit of a sandy beach on one of the islands. Crooks Island, I see from the chart. I point us that way and keep going. It's a bit awkward, rowing with such a strong wind on our beam, but within half an hour I'm pulling Jagular up on the tiny beach. Out on the open water the waves are crashing over the Hiesordt Rocks and sending up glistening arcs of spray like flashes of light, the wind tearing the waves of McBean Channel into jumbled whitecaps and breakers. It feels good to be safely ashore. In a few hours it'll all probably die down and we can continue our journey.

Leaving Jagular on the beach, I set off on foot along the southern shore of the island. We're at the northern edge of a long stretch of open water here, which makes Crooks Island seem far more remote than it is. In reality, we're less than five miles from a major highway—six or seven miles out of Spanish—but, as always, islands offer a sense of isolation and solitude all out of proportion with the distances involved. It's one of the things I like best about this kind of sailing. I feel like a castaway setting out to explore.

With that thought in mind, I decide to continue my walk all the way around the island. It's pleasant going through widely scattered pines, over sweeping slabs of granite, listening to the crash of waves on the rocks just offshore. On the north side of the island I find a sandy bay lined with cliffs and can't resist jumping in, again and again, diving deep into the clear water among the jumbled boulders at the bottom of the cliffs. Then I swim far out into the bay, a mile or more, and float around on my back staring up at the sky. This far out it's still wavy; the wind must still be blowing hard down McBean Channel.

Eventually I complete my circuit of Crooks Island, arriving back at the boat. I suppose I should reef the sail before heading out. And then I remind myself: what for? We're not on any schedule to reach the Benjamin Islands. We don't have to go out again at all today if we don't want to. Do I *want* to go out again?

No, I decide, and feel the last of my self-imposed pressure to keep moving fall away. I'm free—*really* free. It's taken me ten days, but I've made it. This must be how Milton's devilish anti-hero felt when he began his rebellion: released from all strictures and obligations, no longer subject to anyone's judgment but his own.

How much of our lives ashore are simple patterns of unquestioning habit and convention, after all, roles imposed and evaluated by shallow circumstance? We live under a heavy burden of unwritten rules and expectations, caught up in a busy clatter of consumption that allows no time for self-reflection, or self-direction. It's only when shorebound habits and routines have become irrelevant, as they have for me here on Crooks Island, that we find the freedom to create ourselves anew. Maybe that, more than anything else, is the purpose of sailing. An opportunity to shed the habitual selves we inhabit ashore and create something better to replace them. A kinder, more patient self, I hope, one that sweeps along through life on a flood of wonder and gratitude, freed from the web of petty resentments that so often drags us down. For patience, and wonder—and gratitude above all—are the feelings that such slow, uncomplicated sailing evokes. The trick, I suppose, will be holding onto those feelings once we return ashore.

Laughing quietly at the simplicity of it all, I find a pocket of flat sandy shore just big enough to hold the tent and set up camp. Then I pull out one of the British novels I got in the Turnbulls. After reading a few more chapters, hoping in vain for something to happen, I get up and dig through my supplies to see what I can have for supper. I end up celebrating my newfound freedom by having *two* cans of Chef Boyardee lasagna.

◆   ◆   ◆

The next day begins the way so many days here in the North Channel begin: flat calm, cool air, and scattered clouds. The weather forecast, though, is calling for winds of twenty-five knots by this evening, and even more wind tomorrow: thirty knots. We'll have to find somewhere good to hole up for a couple of days, because the only place we'd be going in thirty-knot winds is right to the bottom. Spurred on by grim visions of eight-foot seas and howling gales, I push for an early start from Crooks Island.

It feels early, anyway—I haven't looked at my watch since Beardrop Harbour, so I have no idea what time it is. I'm not even sure what *day* it is. Daylight and darkness have become the only measures of time that matter, wind and wave the only measures of motion. The unthinking, arbitrary routines of life ashore have washed away completely, leaving only a sudden stark simplicity that rises within me like a rocky, sun-lit shoal revealed by a falling tide.

We head east from Crooks Island, into the dawn, running the channel north of Eagle Island on a light westerly breeze. And then, in the pale clean light of morning, we turn south through the scattered rocks and coves of Fox Island and, far-ther south, the Benjamins. We're almost there. I run Jagular up beside a rocky slab just off the southwestern tip of Fox Island and tie up in a natural slip carved into the bedrock, where I step up onto the bare rock for a better look.

Soon, though, I climb back aboard and start sailing again, too eager to delay long. It's a little windier now, so we're mak-ing good time as we cut through the maze of granite slabs and boulders that surround the islands. We're sailing through a rock-studded lagoon just north of North Benjamin Island when a group of kayakers camped on a broad slab of bright granite spots us. They wave, and beckon, and cajole, trying to convince us to come ashore and share their ongoing break-fast: pancakes and biscuits and omelets, sausages and bacon,

*We cut through the maze of granite slabs and boulders
that surround the islands.*

cornbread and fresh fruit, all kinds of food—good food—that I never have aboard Jagular. There are four or five kayaks pulled up on the rock, three or four tents, two or three stoves, a couple of Dutch ovens, a coffee pot, and a campfire, all crowded along the narrow island. It all seems like a lot of bother to me, but everyone is milling around quite cheerfully, talking and laughing, flipping pancakes and sneaking bits of bacon, stirring batter, drinking coffee, making jokes and trading insults, and getting in and out of each other's way like people who have had a lot of practice at it.

"Come on in," they call out, all eager smiles and bright laughter, Gore-Tex jackets and Chaco sandals, fleece vests and Tilley hats. "Yes, come in, come in. We've got plenty of food!"

"Tie me to the mast," I tell the boat. "Stuff my ears with wax." I'm already turning their way.

"Pathetic," Jagular says. "It was one thing when the big boats tried to feed us, but kayakers now?"

"Well, we don't have to take anything," I tell him. "I'm not really hungry, anyway." But I pull in and spend a few minutes chatting with them just the same. They're a cheery bunch, a half dozen paddlers travelling together on their annual North Channel outing. They snap a few photos of Jagular—sailboats his size are definitely a novelty here—and I take a few group photos for them; then we're on our way again.

Before long we make landfall on the western shore of North Benjamin Island, where I find more cliffs to jump off—the best jumping-off rocks of the whole trip, actually, ten or twelve feet high over clear, deep water. The Benjamins are all I've been hoping for, bright sun and blue skies and smooth pink granite slabs interrupted by gnarled pines and wide patches of ripe blueberries. But I haven't seen any safe anchorages or beaches for Jagular yet, and I haven't forgotten the weather forecast—twenty-five knots by evening, thirty knots or more tomorrow. Soon we're sailing southward again along the western side of North Benjamin Island, looking for a safe haven.

◆   ◆   ◆

The main anchorage for the Benjamin Islands, it turns out, is the semi-sheltered cove between North Benjamin and South Benjamin, which must be the place people are thinking of when they say that the Benjamins have been loved to death. The bay is overrun with huge powerboats all jostling and thumping over the waves like fat, well-groomed cattle milling aimlessly around a feedlot. They're the size of two or three-story houses, these boats. One of them cuts across our bow at speed, its huge tumbling wake almost filling our cockpit. They probably didn't even notice us. I'd complain, but I'm too busy eyeing the scantily clad beauties on their foredeck to be angry about it.

"That's the thing about these stupid powerboats," I tell Jagular. "They always seem to be hauling around a bunch of beautiful young women. Not that I'm complaining about that," I add hastily, watching one of them rise to her feet and stretch luxuriously. "Not exactly, anyway. But I'd like to know why you never see those kind of women on sailboats."

"It's not the boat, it's the skipper," Jagular says. "I always have at least one or two of them lounging around on my fore-deck when you're not there."

"You do not!"

"Believe what you want to believe."

Then another wake hits us with a crash, half filling the cockpit with water. By the time I'm done bailing, the power-boat and its beautiful young women are gone. We continue on down past the anchorage, along the east side of South

Benjamin Island. The wind hasn't really started to pick up yet, but it won't be much longer. It must be almost noon already.

Finally, at its southern tip, South Benjamin Island breaks up into a maze of granite domes, steep-walled fjords, and twisting, rocky channels interrupted by huge boulders that rise from the water like the backs of breaching whales. All along the rocky shores, tall pines shift slowly in the wind as if the island itself is breathing quietly beneath them, and thickets of blueberry bushes glistening with fat berries sweep in wide swaths across the rock. It's beautiful—and we'll be sure to find shelter in there somewhere. I drop the rig and row in through a narrow gap between two cliffs. We come out in a perfectly sheltered cove nestled in the junction of three or four rocky islets.

There are other boats moored here, too, tied off bow and stern to huge ring bolts driven into the rock—a trawler yacht, a catamaran, and two or three sailboats. I row past, then drag Jagular up onto a gently sloping slab of rock on the other side of the channel. We're here. We've made it to the Benjamin Islands.

◆   ◆   ◆

One of the sailboats anchored in the cove, it turns out, belongs to a writer I've exchanged a few emails with in the past year, a woman whose stories about sailing the North Channel in her boat *Raggedy Annie* inspired me to come here in the first place. Until I read about her cruises, I barely knew that the North Channel existed. Now, less than a year later, here we are. I actually tried to look her up at her home on Drummond Island before setting out on our trip. That didn't work out—she had already left for another summer of cruising the North Channel—but now I've run into her here. It's another stroke of luck.

"God knows you have more than your share," Jagular says. I can't argue with him. We've had nothing but good fortune, really, since the Turnbulls at least. And even farther back than that.

I spend half an hour chatting with the writer and her friends. As the conversation winds down, she invites me to a potluck supper with them later that evening. I'm about to accept her invitation when I suddenly realize I have nothing at all worth contributing. Ramen noodles? Canned lasagna? Half a package of stale Raspberry Newtons? I can imagine the awkward silences, the sidelong glances, the fragile veneer of politeness tacked over the underlying disgust.

"Well, only…there's that forecast for thirty-knot winds tomorrow," I say. "If I don't leave now, I'll be stuck here for at least two more days."

She looks around—the bright sun, the tall pines, the beautiful rocky islands—and back at me. "Would that be so terrible?" she asks, smiling gently.

But I can't do it. I'm suddenly ashamed of the squalor I've imposed on myself for this trip, the lack of real food, and I refuse to let anyone else see it. I'd rather leave now than bring a pack of Ramen noodles to their dinner.

"I wish I could, but I'm kind of on a schedule. I'm going to head down to Clapperton Island tonight."

She nods politely, accepting my excuse without entirely believing it; it's not her nature to push. "Well, then," she tells me. "Watch out for the southern end of Clapperton—it's quite shallow there, and rocky. You don't want to be there in any kind of waves." She looks at Jagular and smiles again. "And good on you for sailing your little boat this far. All the way from Michigan! That must feel good."

I climb aboard, beaming. It *does* feel good. It feels good not only to have accomplished it, but to have someone I respect, someone who understands sailing and small boats, acknowledge the achievement. I almost feel like I've been knighted.

Still smiling, I wave a casual goodbye and hoist the sail smartly up the mast—backwards.

◆   ◆   ◆

It takes us hours to bash our way to windward down the west side of Clapperton Island. The wind builds steadily the whole way—the cold spray has me in my drysuit again—and when we finally give up and run up on the beach of tiny, flat, wind-scoured Leewin Island, I'm almost tempted to set up the tent and stay there for the night. But it wouldn't be just for the night—we'll be ashore all day tomorrow, too. The grim thought of being stuck on Leewin Island for the next thirty-six hours convinces me to drag the boat back into the water and press on southward.

The wind is strong enough now—still a headwind—that trying to sail would be pointless. Instead, I pull out the oars and row slowly southward, wishing once again that I hadn't used cheap pinned oars from the hardware store. It's impossible to feather the blades because the pins lock them in place, and the wind pushes hard against the oars every time I raise them from the water. That makes rowing, too, almost an exercise in futility. But just up ahead, Vankoughnet Island pinches in close to Clapperton, and I'm betting that somewhere in there we'll find shelter.

Sure enough, there's a sandy beach at the edge of the narrow pass between Vankoughnet Island and Clapperton Island. It's marked "Indian Channel" on my chart. Another ambush site, I suppose. No big boats could ever get in here—the tips of the oars were practically dragging across the rocky bottom with each stroke as I rowed across the bay north of the island—but it's perfect for us. I drag Jagular up onto shore and set up the tent among the abundant poison ivy. Then I settle in to re-read Mark Twain's *Life on the Mississippi.*

The next day the promised winds arrive, and I'm glad we're safely ashore. We wouldn't survive more than a few minutes in this—the bay north of Indian Channel is a tumbling mass of breaking waves. I swim across the narrow gap to Clapperton Island and walk down to Sandfield Point at the southern tip. From here I can look westward into the wind, toward Manitoulin Island and Gore Bay, where we'll be heading next. The entire southern end of Clapperton Island is a chaotic terror of spray and breaking waves, with a wide stretch of jagged boulders half-buried in the waves, and the booming thunder of the surf echoing all along the shore. I've heard stories about boats—big ones—being wrecked in the Clapperton Channel, the shallow pass between Clapperton and Manitoulin Island. Now that I'm here, I have no doubt the stories are true. Finally, with nothing better to do, I swim back to Vankoughnet Island and crawl into the tent to read some more.

◆   ◆   ◆

By the next day the winds have calmed down enough to let us move on. This will be the first real test of our windward ability. From here we'll be heading almost due west along the northern shore of Manitoulin Island, then Cockburn Island, for the next fifty miles. With the prevailing westerly and northwesterly winds, I'm not convinced we can make it. If we can't make decent progress with today's westerly breeze, we may have to give up and sail back to Spanish so I can catch a bus back to Michigan instead.

It's a bit tricky beating upwind through the boulder-fields south of Vankoughnet Island. I've cut across far to the north of the actual channel to save time, past a single rockstrewn island that rises forlornly from the waves, but eventually we make it into open water again and start sailing toward Gore Bay.

"We didn't exactly make it," Jagular protests. "You had to get out and drag me through the rocks for two hundred yards."

"That's what drysuits are for."

"You gave up on sailing and relied on brute force instead," Jagular says. "And yet you complain whenever someone turns on an engine."

"That's different," I insist.

"How?"

"It just is," I tell him.

Either way, we're through the rocks and heading southwest through open water, toward Gore Bay. It's a tough beat to windward. There are a few big keelboats out—they're actually sailing!—and even they look like they're working hard to get anywhere, heeled well over, sails sheeted in tight, spray flying. The waves are big enough that we have to time our tacks just right or we slam to a stop without making it around, but I'm happily surprised to see that we're still making progress. Slowly.

Still, seven or eight miles later—some of them, I admit, under oars—we manage to round the headland on the eastern edge of Gore Bay, where we're able to turn due south. Here the westerly wind bends southward along the tall bluffs, sweeping us down toward the head of the bay on a wild run. In less than an hour we've arrived at the town of Gore Bay. There's a marina up ahead, but I run Jagular up onto the beach at a public park instead, remembering the visitor dock back at Blind River. Then I peel off my drysuit and step ashore.

"We're going to make it," I tell the boat. "Prevailing westerlies or not, we're going to make it back to De Tour Village under sail."

"You rowed half the way here, which is hardly 'under sail,'" Jagular points out. "And we only came seven miles. At that rate it'll take us at least ten more days."

"So?"

"You've only got three packs of Ramen noodles and four Raspberry Newtons left."

"I better go buy some groceries, then," I say. I dig out my wallet from the watertight compartment in the bow and, leaving the boat on the sand beside a pack of screaming children, I walk across the beach, through the park, and into town.

◆ ◆ ◆

I end up spending more than I planned: besides my groceries, I buy a sandwich at a downtown pub, a half dozen used books from the library, a pizza from a dockside restaurant, and best of all, reserve a cozy room in Martha's Inn, a bed and breakfast perched high above the harbor on a steep hill. None of this would be worth mentioning if I had driven into Gore Bay, but because I've arrived here by sea, and am wandering through town on foot and completely anonymous, it all feels like an adventure. I've become a *transient* again, a role I haven't played since we first arrived in Canada, way back in Hilton Beach.

After checking in and paying for my room, I head back to the park and, shooing the screaming children aside, row Jagular into the marina, pulling him up on an out-of-the-way stretch of lawn. Then I go off in search of someone who will give me permission to leave him there overnight. The trick is finding the right person to ask. I head for one of the teenage dock workers.

"Do you mind if I leave my boat there?" I ask.

It's an omnipresent element of marina culture, this teen labor force. Even the individual components don't change much. They're always dressed in yellow polo shirts and khaki shorts, with handheld radios clipped to their belts, and they're always incredibly busy doing a hundred things at once. This one is selling bags of ice, giving directions into town (the marina is right on the downtown waterfront, but people are still asking), assigning slips, and handing out the combination to the bathrooms. Meanwhile he's recommending restaurants, giving out change for the laundry machines, greeting newly arrived boaters, and answering calls on his radio. I know he's not going to have time to ask his boss about leaving my boat on the lawn. He'll just make up an answer—probably "yes," because that will be the easiest way to make me go away. Besides, why should he care? At least I'll stop bothering him. And if he says no, I'll ask the girl at the fuel dock, or the boy mowing the lawn. Eventually I'll get the answer I'm looking for.

But he barely glances at Jagular before answering. "Sure," he says. "That should be all right." Then his radio squawks to life, and he turns away to answer it.

"You're all set," I tell Jagular. "See you in the morning."

◆　　　◆　　　◆

Breakfast is usually the best part of staying at a bed and breakfast. I'm looking forward to it: hot buttered toast, fresh squeezed orange juice, silver dollar pancakes, crisp bacon. But breakfast is at 8:00 a.m. and the weather forecast is calling for southeast winds.

Southeast winds! If we leave right now, at six-thirty, we can be well on our way back to De Tour Village by evening. And tomorrow may bring stiff headwinds again. Headwinds for the next week, for all I know. I scribble a hasty note to Martha and leave it on the table, then head off down the hill to the marina. I manage to grab a glass of orange juice, at least.

It's still calm enough that I have to row out of Gore Bay, but by the time we reach the lighthouse at Janet Head, a faint southeast wind arrives. I hoist sail and head out into the open water, steering a direct course well offshore, past Julia Bay and Barrie Island, out past the Heron Patch shoal and straight toward Cape Robert, fifteen miles west.

"Do you think that's wise?" Jagular asks. "If the wind dies down later we'll be stranded way out there."

"Nonsense," I tell him. "The shortest distance between two points is a straight line, remember?"

It only takes about four hours to row in to Cape Robert later that evening when the wind dies. We're ashore almost before dark.

◆　　　◆　　　◆

The next day is a rollicking tumble through the waves on a strong southeast wind—but this one stays with us all day. We sail at full speed past Vidal Bay, the self-steering lines handling the boat, and the sheet cleated off with a slippery hitch so I can pull out the chart and track our progress. We're actually west of Blind River now, I see. Well over halfway home. The closer we get, the more eager I am to finish our journey. Not that I want it to be over, exactly, but I'm looking forward to a triumphant return, a closed circle, an ending. We'll have accomplished something. Not that anyone else will care, but it seems important to me, at least.

The wind keeps blowing, strong but not too strong, and we sail on past Chamberlain Point, Meldrum Bay, and Twenty Minute Point. Then Meldrum Point, at the very tip of Manitoulin Island. It's evening now, and we'll have to stop soon, but not just yet—Cockburn Island lies just up ahead, across the broad Mississagi Strait, and I can't resist putting Manitoulin Island behind us while the wind is good. We continue on, bashing merrily through the waves on a wind that's carrying us closer and closer to home. Soon we're way out in the middle of the strait, a hundred miles of open water to the south and the sun sinking low. But we're moving fast, and soon we'll be safely ashore on Cockburn Island. It should be our last Canadian landfall of the trip.

I pull out the chart to start looking for a place to camp once we get there. Summer days are long in these latitudes, but we've been out a long time, and have already come twenty-five miles, maybe, with another four or five to go. We're not going to have a lot of light left by the time we reach Cockburn Island. I bend closer to see the chart better in the fading light. Suddenly I start to laugh. We're sailing due west, toward a bulging headland on Cockburn Island's northeastern tip—a headland called the Devil's Horn.

I'm sure I'll feel right at home.

Unlawful Entry

"THIS IS STUPID," I tell the boat the next morning, looking over the chart. "Once we cross False Detour Channel today, we'll be back in U.S. waters. We won't be allowed to land until we've cleared Customs."

"I thought you liked clearing Customs," Jagular says. "All that nonsense about being an international voyager, the master of a vessel—that's what you said back at Hilton Beach."

"Yeah, but the only port of entry back into the U.S. is here—" I put my index finger on the northern edge of Drummond Island—"at Drummond Island Yacht Haven."

"So?"

I make a V with my fingers and check the distance against the chart's scale of miles, then walk my fingers over the chart like a pair of dividers to measure our course.

"It's forty or fifty miles, maybe more," I announce. "And that's straight-line distance. We'll probably have to sail sixty or seventy miles, knowing how well you go to windward. That's two or three days at least."

I measure again, a little more carefully this time. Still about fifty miles. Maybe a little shorter if we go north around Drummond Island instead of south, but either way we're not going to make it in a day, or even two days. I don't even *want* to make it in a day. We're cruising, not racing. And I've already seen the north side of Drummond Island—I'd rather take the southern route back.

"Typical," I say. "A one-size-fits-all set of rules that we're all expected to accept, quietly and without complaint. No questions. No exceptions. And every rule, every procedure, every policy, is designed for the convenience of a machine-driven bureaucracy operating on an industrial scale. There are no allowances made for anyone who chooses to live differently. No dissent is tolerated, and no appeal possible. No understanding that this stupid rule doesn't work for someone in a fourteen-foot boat."

"It's typical, all right," Jagular says. "All you do is complain. You'd rather stand on the margins and hurl useless protests at everything you don't like than join in and try to make things better. It's no surprise you're so discontented—you're completely disengaged from society."

"Nonsense," I tell him. "I engage by voicing dissent—*Vox clamantis in deserto*—reminding people that meek submission to the indignities heaped upon them is not their only option."

"You're an idiot."

I shrug. "Prophets are never respected in their home town."

"That's because they're obnoxious, pathologically eccentric freaks who make no effort to fit in. They'd rather criticize than contribute. That's you, all right: a home-made sailboat for a cave, Ramen noodles instead of locusts and honey, and a willingness to tell everyone else what they're doing wrong. This Customs rule would work fine if you had bothered to set things up so you could sleep aboard. All you'd have to do is throw out an anchor each night and rig a tarp over the cockpit." He pauses. "Except that you left all those screw tips sticking out when you added the new butt block—couldn't be bothered to find shorter screws, I suppose."

"I'm not going to stay offshore for three days anyway," I insist. "No toilet, for one thing. Besides, it's a matter of principle. I refuse to obey such a stupid rule. I'm with Thoreau—civil disobedience is the highest form of civic duty."

"You have to get arrested, then," Jagular says. "That's the whole point of civil disobedience. Gandhi, Martin Luther King—they weren't trying to get away with anything; they were trying to bring attention to unjust laws and force a crisis of conscience. Thoreau, too; he was arrested when he refused to pay his taxes as a protest against the federal government's support of slavery."

"Yeah, but his mother bailed him out, and someone else paid his fine. Thoreau went home the next day and wrote 'Civil Disobedience' and never spent another night in jail. I'll just save my mom the trouble and write my essay now. Same thing."

"Lead on, Mahatma," the boat mutters.

◆   ◆   ◆

The passage across False Detour Channel, from Cockburn Island to Drummond, is almost a repeat of our Mississagi Strait crossing a day earlier—the wind on our beam, a four or five mile hop to the next island, and Lake Huron opening off to the south in an expanse of water so wide that the far shore is lost beneath the horizon. But despite the exposure, it's an easy crossing. Soon we're back in U.S. waters, across the invisible border again.

As I've been hoping, the eastern side of Drummond Island is completely undeveloped—no homes or cottages, and no real roads. There's only a mixed forest of hardwoods, spruces, and cedars, and a long stretch of flat limestone slabs piled up haphazardly all along the water's edge, as if a carefully laid stone wall dividing water from land has collapsed all at once into the waves, leaving a jumble of blocks that stretches for miles. The contrast between the clear blue-green water and the bright white stone is striking. I drag

Jagular up onto the rocks, take off my drysuit, and set off north to explore.

"Remember, we're criminals now," I tell the boat. "Don't get caught. And don't go anywhere."

"That's why most people tie the painter off to something when they land," Jagular calls. I'm already fifty yards up the stony beach. Somewhere nearby is Pilot Cove, an obscure small boat anchorage tucked into a corner of Siltgreaves Bay. I want to check it out on foot before I decide if it's worth beating our way up there.

It's perfect—a narrow pass through the rocks, a natural harbor completely sheltered from all directions, shady tent sites beneath tall pines. But it's overrun with people wearing camouflage shorts, baseball caps from auto parts stores, and T-shirts advertising beer. The nearby bluffs at Marble Head, I remember reading somewhere, are supposed to be a popular destination for offroaders. Some of them, at least, have found their way here. The best harbor on the entire island and not a boat in sight. With a sigh, I turn back.

"No good?" Jagular asks.

"Too good," I tell him. "Everyone else got there first."

I drag the boat off the rocks, row out a ways, and raise the sail. We'll have to head south and hope to find a place to camp farther down the channel. But as I'm tightening the downhaul, the wind dies away completely.

"Crime, apparently, does not pay," the boat says.

"Nonsense," I tell him. "We had plenty of calms before we became criminals, too."

I drop the sails and set out the oars. But as I start rowing, a smothering rush of gray clouds rolls in from the north and a cold drizzling rain, a grim and unforgiving all-day rain, begins to fall. Thunder echoes faintly in the skies like the slow rumble of laughter from somewhere overhead.

◆　　　◆　　　◆

Eventually we come ashore along a flat nondescript marshy stretch of land, where I drag Jagular up onto some rocks and set up the tent in the rain. A soggy night ashore, and a late start the next morning. Still cold. Still raining. A strong southerly wind is sweeping up False Detour Channel. I pull out the oars and start rowing without even bothering to try and beat our way into it. In a couple of miles we'll be able to turn west along the south shore of Drummond Island, and we'll have the wind on our beam.

But by the time we reach the southern edge of the island and make our turn west, the wind has died away completely. Grumbling, I keep rowing. Now the leftover swells from this morning's wind are rolling us—left, right, down, up, awkward lurches that throw off my rhythm and cut our speed in half.

"And we were never that fast to begin with," I complain.

"Why in the world would you build a sailboat if you wanted to go fast?"

Good point. I remind myself to review that question closely when we get home. Meanwhile the southern shore of Drummond Island drags on for ten, twelve, fifteen miles. On the chart, the island looks like a glob of wet paint sliding slowly southward, the runs and drips forming a series of bays and inlets and jutting peninsulas all along the southern shore. Bass Cove. Little Shelter Bay. Big Shoal Cove. Scammon Cove. Traverse Point. Warners Cove. Huron Bay. Fifteen miles of cold rain and rolling, windless slop.

But there's nothing else to do, so I keep rowing. I'm soaked by now—my two-dollar thrift store raincoat is not as waterproof as I had hoped it would be. Cold. Shivering violently. We're barely making any progress at all.

"Remember," Jagular says. "This is supposed to be an adventure, not a ladies' garden party."

"Today I'd take the garden party," I say. But instead the rain continues, and the long slow hours drag on. We keep lurching uncomfortably through the wet and cold, each stroke taking us ten feet closer to the car.

"Try six feet," Jagular says.

Six, then. A thousand strokes per nautical mile. Twenty miles to De Tour Village. Twenty thousand strokes.

"One," I announce, pulling at the oars. "Two…"

◆   ◆   ◆

Then up ahead, at the head of yet another inlet, tied to a floating dock a little way out from shore—I stop rowing and rub the rain from my eyes to be sure. It's Hugh's boat, the wooden-hulled sharpie from Beardrop Harbour. There's no mistaking it. Hugh's house must be somewhere along here, too. I've found it, despite the vague directions that I hardly bothered to remember. I turn to look westward again, down the southern side of Drummond Island. Then back at the sharpie.

"We have an invitation, after all," I tell Jagular. "Stop by on your way back, he said."

"People *say* that all the time."

I look around. The rain is still falling. No sign of clearing skies. Still cold. Nowhere to go. Nothing to do when we get there.

"Hell with it," I tell the boat, and turn us toward shore. "I'm going to pretend that he meant it." Soon we're pulling up on the rocks beside Hugh's house.

"Mooching off the big boats again," Jagular says. "Some adventure."

◆   ◆   ◆

A night ashore with friends, out of the rain, and the world is a brighter place the next morning. The sun seems warmer. The sky bluer. Still not much wind, but yesterday's rolling waves are gone. I row away from Hugh's place, waving happily. Less than twenty miles to go. Our journey is almost over.

But the day stays flat and windless, and by early afternoon I've given up. We're not in that much of a hurry anyway. I row ashore into another of the endless bays and inlets and drag Jagular up onto the rocks. An occasional house or cottage has started to pop up along the shore in the last few miles; if we continue on, we may end up camping in someone's back yard.

"Why would that bother you? That's what we did our first night out," Jagular says.

"We were shipwrecked then. It's an unwritten rule of the sea that castaways are allowed to camp wherever they want. It'd be poor style to do it now."

"It was poor style then," the boat grumbles. I ignore him.

The next morning we're up early, struggling west against light headwinds. It takes us until mid-afternoon to edge past Espanore Island and into Whitney Bay, but it's not far now. Already I can see the tall offshore lighthouse marking the southern end of De Tour Passage, the main shipping lane leading up the St Marys River and through the locks into Lake Superior. One after another, huge red-hulled ore boats—thousand-foot Great Lakes freighters—appear on the horizon, slipping past the light and converging on De Tour Passage for the run north.

With luck, we can clear Customs on Drummond Island tonight, and sail back to De Tour Village tomorrow. If the wind picks up, that is; crossing Whitney Bay it drops away to almost nothing and I'm rowing again. But just as we reach the southern end of De Tour Passage, a new wind sweeps in from the south, putting us on a dead run up De Tour Passage. The sudden wind has come on so strongly that I should probably tie in a reef.

"Fortune favors the bold," Jagular says.

"I liked it more when you gave *good* advice," I tell him. "Ignoring it brought so much satisfaction."

But I leave the sail unreefed anyway. After three days of light airs and calms I can't resist the sudden speed. It's only six or seven miles to Sims Point, where we'll be able to turn east under the lee of Drummond Island. And we still have five or six miles to go after that. If we don't get there in time to clear Customs tonight, we'll have to find somewhere to camp—illegally—right where we're most likely to be seen. So I ease the sheet until the boom is squared right out, and we're off and running down the channel.

A couple of big sloops, thirty-footers, come motoring in behind us—and they're not gaining on us. It's getting windier as we surf along, surging forward with a sudden acceleration as each wave slides beneath us, and the big boats behind us keep dropping farther and farther back. We're right at the edge of a gybe and broach, but we're moving so fast I decide to keep going anyway. We sail past De Tour Village at full speed, dodging around the Drummond Island ferry with a couple of quick gybes, and on around Sims Point and into Potagannissing Bay.

"There—we've crossed our outbound path," I tell the boat. "Our circumnavigation is complete." For a minute I'm tempted to turn back westward and avoid the fifteen-mile detour to Drummond Island Yacht Haven and back. We could sail right into the De Tour Village harbor on a beam reach with this wind. We'd be ashore in less than an hour. From there it'd be a twenty-minute walk to the car. Throw the boat on the trailer, and we could be on our way home tonight.

"Without clearing Customs," Jagular says.

"Yeah, but does anybody really check that stuff? Who keeps records of all that?"

"One way to find out."

I look back once more at De Tour Village. It's tempting. Then again, by the time I *do* find out, it'll be too late. Never underestimate bureaucracy's enthusiasm for persecution, I remind myself. The first priority of every institution is to preserve its own authority by imposing a series of pointless and arbitrary demands, and punishing those who resist.

"No, my scofflaw past is behind me," I tell Jagular. "I'm a law-abiding citizen now, a productive member of society with a valid passport and an official clearance number from Canadian Customs."

"Which you lost," the boat points out.

"I didn't lose it. It just got wet and kind of fell apart. Anyway, you're right about needing to fit in better with the rest of society. We'll do our re-entry by the book, t's crossed and i's dotted."

"Without mentioning that we've been camping ashore illegally for the past three nights."

"What they don't know will never hurt them," I say.

◆   ◆   ◆

Just after sunset we come whipping into Drummond Island Yacht Haven on a fast broad reach. I ease the tiller over to make the turn into the harbor without losing speed, sheeting in hard to angle between the crowded docks on a beam reach, and slip past the rows of big sloops and fat powerboats sitting alone and neglected in their slips, shiny chrome and plastic boats with names like *Second Wind II* and *Midas Touch* and *Never Again III*. I sail right past them all in my three-hundred-dollar Pirate Racer, heading straight for the boat ramp at the end of the marina. Ten yards out I let the sheet fly, and Jagular glides gently up the ramp. I hop out and pull the boat farther onto shore, then set out to find the Customs office.

CLOSED, the sign on the door says. HOURS OF OPERATION: 12 p.m. TO 9 p.m.

I press my face up against the window. Inside the small room are two desks and some file cabinets. A clock on the wall reads 9:21 p.m.

I look around, but the parking lot is empty. There's no one here. Another note on the door gives a toll-free number to call for late arrivals. I read it over a few times until I have the number memorized, then head off to look for a pay phone. Just across the parking lot, outside the marina office—also closed—I find one. I pick up the receiver, ready to punch in the number.

No dial tone. I click the lever a few times, then listen again. Still nothing. I enter the number just in case, but nothing happens. With a sigh, I head back to the boat ramp.

"What kind of stupid Customs office gives you a number to call but no phone?" I ask the boat. "Not only are their rules stupid, but, like bureaucracies everywhere, they're doing their best to make it impossible to do what they ask anyway."

"It wouldn't be impossible if you got a cell phone like everyone else."

"Mindless conformity is always easier than thinking for yourself," I say. "That doesn't make it any more appealing."

"So now anyone with a cell phone is a mindless conformist?"

I stomp off without answering. Maybe there's someone aboard one of the boats who has a cell phone I can use. And there is—an elderly couple on an ugly cabin cruiser with *GAIL FORCE* painted on the transom. The woman (Gail, I assume) holds out her phone gingerly, the way she'd hand over her purse to a mugger. I have to ask her to show me how to turn the stupid thing on—there are buttons everywhere—and then I punch in the number. Nothing happens.

"You have to hit *SEND*," Gail tells me, looking over my shoulder.

Still nothing.

"I almost never get a signal here," she adds.

I hand the phone back to her with a hurried thank you and stomp off again. I walk up and down the docks for twenty minutes, but there's no one else around. Nothing else to do. Finally I go back to the boat and row out of the marina—no use hanging around to get caught. Just outside the breakwater there's a sandy beach beside a playground. It'll do. For a moment I even consider anchoring a few feet offshore and sleeping aboard.

But why? I made a reasonable effort to follow their stupid rule, but the game is rigged. You can never do what they want no matter how hard you try. I'm not going take the truly asinine step of anchoring off now, after I've already slept ashore for the past three nights. Maybe tomorrow if I'm feeling ambitious I'll sneak off early before the marina opens, and then come back in pretending that I've just arrived. So the hell with sleeping aboard. Instead I drag Jagular up onto the beach and set up my tent at the edge of the playground, beside the monkey bars.

◆   ◆   ◆

I wake early and climb out of the tent. There's a man unloading a trailer full of kayaks onto the beach, rentals that someone has arranged to be delivered here from an outfitter on the west side of Drummond Island. The weather doesn't look too promising for touring, though. Dark clouds. Lots of wind. I look at the marina flagpole: the flag is snapping briskly, twenty knots out of the west—exactly the direction we'll have to sail to reach De Tour Village after clearing Customs. Too bad we didn't end the trip at De Tour Village last night. Now we'll have to waste half the day waiting around for Customs, then face a tough ten-mile beat back to the car. We probably won't make it in until well after dark. Maybe not until tomorrow. And it looks like it's going to be raining soon, too.

But Customs doesn't open until noon, I remind myself with a smile. And it's not even 7:30 yet.

"You need a hand with those?" I ask the man with the kayaks.

"That'd be great," he says.

After we're done unloading, he thanks me and starts to climb into his truck.

"You wouldn't be heading back to the west side of the island by any chance, would you?" I ask before he can close the door. "Somewhere near the ferry to De Tour Village?"

◆   ◆   ◆

I'm back at the marina with the car and trailer by 11:15, even after stopping for breakfast along the way. By now someone has probably seen the tent, so I stop in at the marina office to ask what I owe for camping in their playground—I don't want to risk losing my new law-abiding status before my interview with Customs even begins.

"What do I owe you for camping here overnight?" I ask the manager.

"Campground's full," he says, not looking up from the stack of papers he's shuffling through. He's got a half-eaten apple fritter in one hand and a half-full cup of coffee on the desk in front of him.

"No, I came in late last night and set my tent up on the lawn over there by the playground," I explain. "How much do I owe you for that?"

"Camping's not allowed on the lawn," he says, still not looking up. "I can rent you one of our cabins, though," he adds without much enthusiasm, then dunks the fritter into the coffee. No looking, no aiming. He's a natural.

"No, I camped here *last* night," I tell him. "On the lawn, over by the playground. There was no one around to ask, but I figured I wouldn't be in anyone's way. Can I give you a little bit to cover that?"

He sets the papers down and turns to look at me, trying to judge how much money I'm likely to spend in his store. Twelve-dollar K-Mart board shorts. Fleece pullover my wife found in a thrift store ten years ago. Teva sandals so worn that I've had to stick one sole together with duct tape.

"Camping's thirty dollars," he says.

Thirty dollars! I was expecting eight dollars, maybe ten. Or, really, I wanted him to be so impressed by my honesty that he'd tell me not to worry about it. I'd buy a soda and a candy bar to give him a little business in return, and we'd both be happy. But no. One night in this stupid marina is going to end up costing me almost twenty percent of my total expenses for the entire three-week trip.

"Wow. Thirty dollars?" I say. "Really? I didn't even use your bathrooms or take a shower or anything."

He stabs the fritter into the coffee again and takes a bite, staring at me the whole time. He doesn't even blink. After a moment, I give up. "Boy, honesty is expensive around here, huh?" I say, pulling out my wallet and handing over the money. I've got four dollars left.

"Bathroom's right over there," he says, waving a hand vaguely toward the yard. "Combination is 5-2-3." He slides my money into the cash register, hands me a receipt, and picks up his papers again. After a moment I realize I've been dismissed.

◆   ◆   ◆

At 11:55 a black and gray Mustang marked Customs Border Patrol pulls into the parking lot. The doors open simultaneously, and an officer steps out on each side. Shiny black boots. Sharply creased black-and-gray CBP uniforms. Flat-brimmed drill sergeant hats. Aviator sunglasses with mirrored lenses. Belts stuffed with all kinds of cop gear, guns and radios and tasers and handcuffs and pepper spray and who knows what else. They stop to survey the scene—one looks left, one right, establishing overlapping fields of fire—and then walk together to the office, long slow steps that crunch loudly across the gravel parking lot like the inexorable march of fate.

"This should be fun," Jagular says.

The officers disappear into the building. At 12:31 the door opens again and one of them comes out and stands in the doorway—he must have lost the coin toss.

"I need to report in from Canada," I tell him.

He eyes me for a moment before answering. My reflection in his sunglasses looks small and oddly shaped and strangely insignificant, like a cringing Quasimodo appealing for mercy he's not likely to receive.

"You got in just now?" he says finally.

"Last night, actually," I tell him. "I tried to use the after-hours number to call in, but the phone wasn't working."

He stares at me some more, then ducks back inside the office and closes the door behind him. After a couple of minutes he steps back out. "You came ashore last night?" he says.

"Yeah. I was trying to check in but I got here a little late." In his sunglasses my reflection seems to shrink even further.

"Did you go anywhere else?" he says.

"No," I tell him. "Just here. I walked around the docks to try to borrow a phone from someone, but—"

"You were walking around the docks?" he says sharply.

"Yeah," I mumble. My reflection is cringing again.

"Anywhere else?" he asks.

"Just here, and along the docks," I say, wishing I were a better liar. From where we're standing, he's aimed directly at my tent, and at Jagular waiting on the beach beside it. The car and trailer I brought over on the ferry from Drummond Island this morning are sitting in the parking lot behind him. But he hasn't even asked what boat I've come in on.

He gives me another long cop stare. "I need to ask you a few questions," he tells me. "Then make some phone calls. Because what you've done here is, you've come ashore without a Customs clearance. That's contamination. And then you walked around the docks and spread the contamination farther. That's the situation. Not good. Wait here." Then he's gone, back inside the office.

For the next four hours, that's the pattern: he comes out of the office to ask a few more questions, reminds me of the severity of my crimes and the seriousness of the resulting contamination, and then disappears back inside for fifteen or twenty minutes. Each time he steps inside I walk back over to the beach to let the boat know how things are going.

"Well?" Jagular says. "How bad is it?"

"Pretty bad," I tell him. "We've contaminated the island. And the mainland, come to think of it, but they haven't found out about that yet."

"It's the Ramen noodles, isn't it?"

I shrug. "Well, I ate the last of the Strawberry Newtons in Gore Bay, so it can't be them."

Back to the office for another round.

"Well, they dropped the criminal trespassing charges after I showed them my receipt for the camping fee," I tell the boat at our next update. "But they're still not sure how far the contamination has spread. So now we're dealing with the prospect of an unknown amount of contamination. They're making more phone calls."

Back again. A few more questions and another scolding.

"Everything's still contaminated," I report to Jagular when I get back to the beach. "And they weren't happy about the speeding ticket I got in 1994. Pursuant to 19 CFR 4.2, I'll be going to prison for five years, and I'll have to pay a $10,000 fine besides."

"Blood from a turnip," Jagular says. "What about me?"

"Confiscated. Any and all conveyances associated with illegal activities are subject to forfeiture and seizure, 8 CFR 235.1."

"Maybe I'll end up with a better captain, at least," Jagular says.

"Yeah, good luck on the auction block," I tell him. "I wouldn't even bid on you myself."

Back to the office. Another few questions and phone calls.

"Well?" the boat says when I return.

"Fingerprints," I tell him, trying to wipe the sticky ink off my hands without much success. "I've been fingerprinted at least four times in the past twenty years, but I guess they wanted to be sure. And after they found out I used to be a high school English teacher, they took away my passport— too much Thoreau, I suppose."

It's been three and a half hours and no one has even glanced at the boat or the tent. There's been no inspection. No quarantine. Not a single question about how I got here. If I were smuggling cocaine, or weapons-grade plutonium, or even a cockpit full of angry jihadists and a few bales of marijuana, I'd have had plenty of time to offload them.

"Maybe we should take up smuggling," I tell the boat. "It doesn't seem like it'd be very hard."

Eventually, though, both officers step out of the office together again. The phone calls and consultations are over. It's time for the inspection. There's a final murmured conversation as they run through their plan one last time, and then my interrogator walks toward me with his long slow steps, head turning this way and that, assessing potential threats. His partner stays behind to provide covering fire.

"Where's your boat?" the officer asks.

"You're looking at it," I tell him.

He turns his head, gives Jagular a long stare. Walks closer and looks down into the cockpit. Eyes the screw tips protruding from the butt joint.

"You went to Canada in this?" he says finally.

I shrug. "It's the only boat I have."

There's another long silence. He walks all the way around the boat. Glances at the tent under the monkey bars. Then he shakes his head, pulls off his Ray-Bans and tucks them in his shirt pocket, and walks back to the office.

◆   ◆   ◆

We're finally released, after four and a half hours of questions and scoldings, and a final stern admonition about the consequences that could have imposed for my crimes. I manage to get the boat on the trailer and the gear tied down just as the thunderstorms that have been hanging on the horizon all day sweep in and the rain starts hammering down. Fifteen minutes later we're pulling on to the ferry back to De Tour Village.

Our trip is over, I realize. The long interrogation has interfered with any sense of closure or resolution. No time to reflect on what we've done, what it might mean. It's a bit of a disappointment. But maybe that's ok, I decide. There's no ending this way—just the promise of future voyages, future adventures. After three weeks aboard, I'm starting to feel like I'm almost a competent sailor. Maybe next year we can keep going, through Georgian Bay and into the Trent-Severn Canal, into Lake Ontario and the Thousand Islands. Down the St. Lawrence to the sea.

By the time the ferry pulls in to De Tour Village, I've got a Jimmy Buffet CD playing and I'm already starting to think about launching from Spanish next year so we can skip the inadvisable western shores, with their forty miles of rocky shoals. That would put us a lot closer to Georgian Bay. And let us avoid clearing Customs altogether. By the time I pull in to buy gas for the drive home, it feels like a definite plan.

"We didn't do too badly," I tell Jagular as I start the pump. "Twenty days. Two hundred and fifty miles, more or less. Nothing broken. No disasters. I'm starting to get the hang of all this. What do you think—Georgian Bay next year?"

"Maybe," the boat says. "If I can't find a better option before then."

I'm screwing the cap back on the gas tank when a battered pick-up pulls in alongside. It's Hugh. He gets out, smiling.

"I thought that must be you," he says. "You made it, huh?"

"Yeah, we did," I tell him. "Had a bit of a run-in with Customs on Drummond Island, but they let us go eventually. Everything else has been great. I thought I might be getting in a bit over my head with this trip when we started, but I feel like I know what I'm doing now. Like I can take care of myself, you know?"

"Sure," Hugh says. "Of course you can." He turns and pulls something out of his truck. "By the way, are these yours?"

He's holding a pair of pants; I must have left them behind when I stayed at his house. I kick the trailer tire unobtrusively before Jagular can say anything.

"Thanks," I tell Hugh. "I didn't even know they were missing."

We talk for a few minutes, and then Hugh gets in and drives off toward Sault Saint Marie. I walk back toward the car, the forgotten pants slung over my shoulder. It's a good thing I ate the last of the Newtons at Gore Bay. They'd be laughing their fool heads off.

"You've still got me, though," Jagular says.

"And you're not going to let me forget about the pants, are you?"

"Those who don't remember the past are doomed to repeat it."

Doesn't sound all that bad, I decide. Some things are worth repeating. I hop in the car, start up the Jimmy Buffet CD again, and pull out onto the highway. Time to go home.

For now, anyway.

Acknowledgments

Many people had a hand in the creation of this book, and I'm grateful for their assistance. Not least among them is Tom McGrath, whose classic *Voyages of the Damn Foole* was, in large part, the inspiration for my Jagular stories. Those who have read McGrath's book—and now mine—know just how indebted I am. If I've echoed even a small part of Tom McGrath's humor and wisdom in these pages, I'll have done very well indeed.

To Patrick Hull, whose generous support came just when it was most needed—thank you.

To my brother Lance, who got me started in the first place, and has stepped in more than once to fix things after I've given up—what can be said except: Thank you. Not nearly enough, I know. But thank you.

Thanks also to:

Chuck "the duck" Leinweber at duckworksmagazine.com and Josh Colvin at *Small Craft Advisor* for their enthusiasm and encouragement through the years; and John Welsford, who interrupted his busy schedule to write the Foreword (and showed me how to get to windward just a bit more efficiently besides).

My fellow writers Eric Hayes, Jason Hess, and Cara Stoddard, who read early drafts and took them seriously; my editor Kate Haas at www.katehaas.com, whose comments and suggestions made this a better book than it would have been otherwise; and Eric Bott, whose drawings capture the spirit of the stories as no photos ever could.

Julie Mckay Covert, who showed me what Kickstarter was all about; and Richard Wynne of Lodestar Books, whose expertise in typesetting and design was desperately needed, and hugely appreciated.

And many thanks indeed to my online backers, who believed that someday a book worth reading would come of all this—without you, it wouldn't have been possible. Among my earliest and most generous supporters at Kickstarter.com were:

Dan Douglas, Cathy Statz, Chuck Pierce, Mitch Salzwedel, Chuck "the duck" Leinweber, Paul Haynie, Tom Martin, Hazel Clark, Benjamin Algera, Craig and Pam Wolfson, Marti Hemwall and John Peterson, Nigel Johnson, Helen Howard, Kathy Schumacher, Josh Ross, Simeon Baldwin, Murray Stevens, Hugh Covert, Bryan Cull, the Kyle and Melissa Tomesh family, Steve Deml, Pehr Jansson, Cameron Eckert, Fred Rappley, Bob Wessel, Alex Wetmore, Jon Hinson, Kristen Kvalheim, Don Hamerla, Christine and Nick Hamele, Steve and Angie Statz, Ross Lillistone, John West, Gary Blankenship, Sarah Lloyd, Michael Nerbovig, Don Kurylko, Chanda Manning, Andrew Barclay, Mario Stoltz, Dick Wynne, Donna Martin, Cara Stoddard, Karen Lemke, Terry Dunn, Dave Mortenson, Jake Lindgren, Jamie Schering, Jim Ballou, Kristen Burkholder, Tom Quinn, Marlene and Ray Pamperin (thanks, Mom and Dad!), Gary Mac, Bruce and Tammy Krings, John and Martha Wright, Mark W. Smith, Norm Takusagawa, and Pam Pamperin.